ANTITRUST

Problems, Text, Cases

2000 Supplement

EDITORIAL ADVISORY BOARD

Aspen Publishers, Inc.
Legal Education Division

Richard A. Epstein
James Parker Hall Distinguished Service Professor of Law
University of Chicago

E. Allan Farnsworth
Alfred McCormack Professor of Law
Columbia University

Ronald J. Gilson
Charles J. Meyers Professor of Law and Business
Stanford University
Marc and Eva Stern Professor of Law and Business
Columbia University

Geoffrey C. Hazard, Jr.
Trustee Professor of Law
University of Pennsylvania

James E. Krier
Earl Warren DeLano Professor of Law
University of Michigan

Elizabeth Warren
Leo Gottlieb Professor of Law
Harvard University

Bernard Wolfman
Fessenden Professor of Law
Harvard University

ANTITRUST ANALYSIS

Problems, Text, Cases
Fifth Edition

2000 Supplement

PHILLIP AREEDA

Late Langdell Professor of Law
Harvard University

LOUIS KAPLOW

Professor of Law
Harvard University

ASPEN LAW & BUSINESS
A Division of Aspen Publishers, Inc.
Gaithersburg   New York

Copyright © 2000 by Aspen Law & Business

All rights reserved. This publication is sold with the understanding that the publisher and authors are not engaged in rendering legal, accounting, or other professional services. If legal advice or other professional assistance is required, the services of a competent professional person should be sought.

No part of this publication may be reproduced or transmitted in any form or by any means, electronic or mechanical, including photocopy, recording, or any information storage and retrieval system, without permission in writing from the publisher. Requests for permission to make copies of any part of this publication should be mailed to:

Permissions
Aspen Law & Business
1185 Avenue of the Americas
New York, NY 10036

Printed in the United States of America

2 3 4 5 6 7 8 9 0

Library of Congress Cataloging-in-Publication Data

Areeda, Philip
    Antitrust analysis : problems, text, cases / Phillip Areeda,
Louis Kaplow. — 5th ed.
    p.   cm.
    Includes index.
    ISBN 1-56706-566-X (casebound)
    ISBN 0-7355-1724-x (supplement)
    1. Antitrust law — United States — Cases.   I. Kaplow,
Louis. II. Title.
KF1648.A7   1997
343.73'0721 — dc21   97-27101
    CIP

About Aspen Law & Business Legal Education Division

With a dedication to preserving and strengthening the long-standing tradition of publishing excellence in legal education, Aspen Law &Business continues to provide the highest quality teaching and learning resources for today's law school community. Careful development, meticulous editing, and an unmatched responsiveness to the evolving needs of today's discerning educators combine in the creation of our outstanding casebooks, coursebooks, textbooks, and study aids.

ASPEN LAW & BUSINESS
A Division of Aspen Publishers, Inc.
A Wolters Kluwer Company
www.aspenpublishers.com

Contents

Table of Cases ix
Preface xi

Chapter 2. Horizontal Restraints: Collaboration Among Competitors 1

2B. Modern Applications: Determining Which Restraints Are Reasonable 1
¶220' Need-Based Educational Aid Antitrust Protection Act of 1997 1
California Dental Association v. Federal Trade Commission 2
¶222' Competition Collaboration Guidelines 22

2E. Concerted Refusals to Deal 23
NYNEX v. Discon 23

Chapter 3. Monopoly 29

3A. Monopolization 29
¶312' Microsoft Litigation 29
United States v. Microsoft Corp. 29
Intel Corp. 70

vii

Contents

Chapter 4. Vertical Restraints   **75**

4A. Restricted Distribution   **75**
State Oil Co. v. Khan   75

Chapter 5. Mergers: Horizontal, Vertical, and Conglomerate   **85**

5D. Horizontal Mergers   **85**
Federal Trade Commission v. Staples   85

Appendix   **113**

Antitrust Guidelines for Collaborations Among Competitors   113

Table of Cases

Italics indicate principal cases. References are to paragraph numbers.

California Dental Association v. Federal Trade Commission, 221'
Federal Trade Commission v. Staples, 527'
Intel Corp. (FTC), 313'
NYNEX v. Discon, 266'
State Oil Co. v. Khan, 407'
United States v. Microsoft Corp., 312'

Preface

This supplement contains major Supreme Court decisions and summarizes other developments subsequent to the publication of Antitrust Analysis, Fifth Edition, in 1997.

The editorial matters stated on pp. xxxvii-xxxviii of Antitrust Analysis are applicable here and will not be repeated. New material bears paragraph numbers keyed to the original. For example, new ¶220' should be considered after ¶220 of the original.

Students and teachers may find it useful to indicate the existence of relevant supplementary material at appropriate points in the original book.

L.K.

June 2000

Chapter 2

Horizontal Restraints: Collaboration Among Competitors

2B. Modern Applications: Determining Which Restraints Are Reasonable

Page 238. At the end of note 30, add the following:

220'. **Need-Based Educational Aid Antitrust Protection Act of 1997.** In 1997, Congress extended until 2001 prior legislation (enacted in the wake of the litigation described in note 30) granting a limited antitrust exemption that allows institutions of higher education at which students are admitted on a need-blind basis to agree to: (1) provide aid on the basis of need only; (2) use common principles of needs analysis; (3) use a common aid application; and (4) exchange a student's financial information through a third party; but the institutions are not permitted to agree on the amount of any prospective financial aid award to a specific individual.

Page 247. After ¶221, add the following:

CALIFORNIA DENTAL ASSOCIATION v. FEDERAL TRADE COMMISSION
119 S. Ct. 1604 (1999)

Justice SOUTER. . . . There are two issues in this case: whether the jurisdiction of the Federal Trade Commission extends to the California Dental Association (CDA), a nonprofit professional association, and whether a "quick look" sufficed to justify finding that certain advertising restrictions adopted by the CDA violated the antitrust laws. We hold that the Commission's jurisdiction under the Federal Trade Commission Act (FTC Act) extends to an association that, like the CDA, provides substantial economic benefit to its for-profit members, but that where, as here, any anticompetitive effects of given restraints are far from intuitively obvious, the rule of reason demands a more thorough enquiry into the consequences of those restraints than the Court of Appeals performed.

I

The CDA is a voluntary nonprofit association of local dental societies to which some 19,000 dentists belong, including about three-quarters of those practicing in the State. . . . The CDA lobbies and litigates in its members' interests, and conducts marketing and public relations campaigns for their benefit.

The dentists who belong to the CDA through these associations agree to abide by a Code of Ethics (Code) including the following §10:

> "Although any dentist may advertise, no dentist shall advertise or solicit patients in any form of communication in a manner that is false or misleading in any material respect. In order to properly serve the public, dentists should represent themselves in a manner that contributes to the esteem of the public. Dentists should not misrepresent their training and competence in any way that would be false or misleading in any material respect."

The CDA has issued a number of advisory opinions interpreting this section,[1] and through separate advertising guidelines intended to help members

---

[1] The advisory opinions, which substantially mirror parts of the California Business and Professions Code, see Cal. Bus. & Prof. Code Ann. §§651, 1680 (West 1999), include the

California Dental Association

comply with the Code and with state law the CDA has advised its dentists of disclosures they must make under state law when engaging in discount advertising.[2]

Responsibility for enforcing the Code rests in the first instance with the local dental societies, to which applicants for CDA membership must submit copies of their own advertisements and those of their employers or referral services to assure compliance with the Code. The local societies also actively seek information about potential Code violations by applicants or CDA members. Applicants who refuse to withdraw or revise objectionable advertisements may be denied membership; and members who, after a hearing, remain similarly recalcitrant are subject to censure, suspension, or expulsion from the CDA.

---

following propositions:
"A statement or claim is false or misleading in any material respect when it:
"a. contains a misrepresentation of fact;
"b. is likely to mislead or deceive because in context it makes only a partial disclosure of relevant facts;
"c. is intended or is likely to create false or unjustified expectations of favorable results and/or costs;
"d. relates to fees for specific types of services without fully and specifically disclosing all variables and other relevant factors;
"e. contains other representations or implications that in reasonable probability will cause an ordinarily prudent person to misunderstand or be deceived.
"Any communication or advertisement which refers to the cost of dental services shall be exact, without omissions, and shall make each service clearly identifiable, without the use of such phrases as 'as low as,' 'and up,' 'lowest prices,' or words or phrases of similar import.
"Any advertisement which refers to the cost of dental services and uses words of comparison or relativity—for example, 'low fees'—must be based on verifiable data substantiating the comparison or statement of relativity. The burden shall be on the dentist who advertises in such terms to establish the accuracy of the comparison or statement of relativity."
"Advertising claims as to the quality of services are not susceptible to measurement or verification; accordingly, such claims are likely to be false or misleading in any material respect."

---

[2] The disclosures include:
"1. The dollar amount of the nondiscounted fee for the service[.]
"2. Either the dollar amount of the discount fee or the percentage of the discount for the specific service[.]
"3. The length of time that the discount will be offered[.]
"4. Verifiable fees[.]
"5. [The identity of] [s]pecific groups who qualify for the discount or any other terms and conditions or restrictions for qualifying for the discount."

¶221

The Commission brought a complaint against the CDA, alleging that it applied its guidelines so as to restrict truthful, nondeceptive advertising, and so violated §5 of the FTC Act. The complaint alleged that the CDA had unreasonably restricted two types of advertising: price advertising, particularly discounted fees, and advertising relating to the quality of dental services. An Administrative Law Judge (ALJ) held the Commission to have jurisdiction over the CDA, which, the ALJ noted, had itself "stated that a selection of its programs and services has a potential value to members of between $22,739 and $65,127." He found that, although there had been no proof that the CDA exerted market power, no such proof was required to establish an antitrust violation under In re Mass. Bd. of Registration in Optometry, 110 F.T.C. 549 (1988), since the CDA had unreasonably prevented members and potential members from using truthful, nondeceptive advertising, all to the detriment of both dentists and consumers of dental services. He accordingly found a violation of §5 of the FTC Act.

The Commission adopted the factual findings of the ALJ except for his conclusion that the CDA lacked market power, with which the Commission disagreed. The Commission treated the CDA's restrictions on discount advertising as illegal per se. In the alternative, the Commission held the price advertising (as well as the nonprice) restrictions to be violations of the Sherman and FTC Acts under an abbreviated rule-of-reason analysis. . . .

The Court of Appeals for the Ninth Circuit affirmed, sustaining the Commission's assertion of jurisdiction over the CDA and its ultimate conclusion on the merits. The court thought it error for the Commission to have applied per se analysis to the price advertising restrictions, finding analysis under the rule of reason required for all the restrictions. But the Court of Appeals went on to explain that the Commission had properly

> "applied an abbreviated, or 'quick look,' rule of reason analysis designed for restraints that are not per se unlawful but are sufficiently anticompetitive on their face that they do not require a full-blown rule of reason inquiry. See *NCAA*. ('The essential point is that the rule of reason can sometimes be applied in the twinkling of an eye.' [Ibid. (citing P. Areeda, The "Rule of Reason" in Antitrust Analysis: General Issues 37-38 (Federal Judicial Center, June 1981) (parenthetical omitted)).] It allows the condemnation of a 'naked restraint' on price or output without an 'elaborate industry analysis.'"

The Court of Appeals thought truncated rule-of-reason analysis to be in order for several reasons. As for the restrictions on discount advertising, they "amounted in practice to a fairly 'naked' restraint on price competition itself."

The CDA's procompetitive justification, that the restrictions encouraged disclosure and prevented false and misleading advertising, carried little weight because "it is simply infeasible to disclose all of the information that is required," and "the record provides no evidence that the rule has in fact led to increased disclosure and transparency of dental pricing." As to non-price advertising restrictions, the court said that

> "[t]hese restrictions are in effect a form of output limitation, as they restrict the supply of information about individual dentists' services. . . . The restrictions may also affect output more directly, as quality and comfort advertising may induce some customers to obtain nonemergency care when they might not otherwise do so . . . . Under these circumstances, we think that the restriction is a sufficiently naked restraint on output to justify quick look analysis."

The Court of Appeals went on to hold that the Commission's findings with respect to the CDA's agreement and intent to restrain trade, as well as on the effect of the restrictions and the existence of market power, were all supported by substantial evidence. In dissent, Judge Real took the position that the Commission's jurisdiction did not cover the CDA as a nonprofit professional association engaging in no commercial operations. But even assuming jurisdiction, he argued, full-bore rule-of-reason analysis was called for, since the disclosure requirements were not naked restraints and neither fixed prices nor banned nondeceptive advertising.

We granted certiorari to resolve conflicts among the Circuits on the Commission's jurisdiction over a nonprofit professional association and the occasions for abbreviated rule-of-reason analysis. We now vacate the judgment of the Court of Appeals and remand.

II

... The FTC Act is at pains to include not only an entity "organized to carry on business for its own profit," 15 U.S.C. §44, but also one that carries on business for the profit "of its members," ibid. While such a supportive organization may be devoted to helping its members in ways beyond immediate enhancement of profit, no one here has claimed that such an entity must devote itself single-mindedly to the profit of others. It could, indeed, hardly be supposed that Congress intended such a restricted notion of covered supporting organizations, with the opportunity this would bring with it for avoiding jurisdiction where the purposes of the FTC Act would obviously call for asserting it.

¶221 *California Dental Association*

Just as the FTC Act does not require that a supporting organization must devote itself entirely to its members' profits, neither does the Act say anything about how much of the entity's activities must go to raising the members' bottom lines. There is accordingly no apparent reason to let the statute's application turn on meeting some threshold percentage of activity for this purpose, or even satisfying a softer formulation calling for a substantial part of the nonprofit entity's total activities to be aimed at its members' pecuniary benefit. To be sure, proximate relation to lucre must appear; the FTC Act does not cover all membership organizations of profit-making corporations without more, and an organization devoted solely to professional education may lie outside the FTC Act's jurisdictional reach, even though the quality of professional services ultimately affects the profits of those who deliver them.

There is no line drawing exercise in this case, however, where the CDA's contributions to the profits of its individual members are proximate and apparent. Through for-profit subsidiaries, the CDA provides advantageous insurance and preferential financing arrangements for its members, and it engages in lobbying, litigation, marketing, and public relations for the benefit of its members' interests. This congeries of activities confers far more than de minimis or merely presumed economic benefits on CDA members; the economic benefits conferred upon the CDA's profit-seeking professionals plainly fall within the object of enhancing its members' "profit," which the FTC Act makes the jurisdictional touchstone. There is no difficulty in concluding that the Commission has jurisdiction over the CDA.

The logic and purpose of the FTC Act comport with this result. The FTC Act directs the Commission to "prevent" the broad set of entities under its jurisdiction "from using unfair methods of competition in or affecting commerce and unfair or deceptive acts or practices in or affecting commerce." Nonprofit entities organized on behalf of for-profit members have the same capacity and derivatively, at least, the same incentives as for-profit organizations to engage in unfair methods of competition or unfair and deceptive acts. It may even be possible that a nonprofit entity up to no good would have certain advantages, not only over a for-profit member but over a for-profit membership organization as well; it would enjoy the screen of superficial disinterest while devoting itself to serving the interests of its members without concern for doing more than breaking even. . . .

We therefore conclude that the Commission had jurisdiction to pursue the claim here, and turn to the question whether the Court of Appeals devoted sufficient analysis to sustain the claim that the advertising restrictions promulgated by the CDA violated the FTC Act.

III

The Court of Appeals treated as distinct questions the sufficiency of the analysis of anticompetitive effects and the substantiality of the evidence supporting the Commission's conclusions. Because we decide that the Court of Appeals erred when it held as a matter of law that quick-look analysis was appropriate (with the consequence that the Commission's abbreviated analysis and conclusion were sustainable), we do not reach the question of the substantiality of the evidence supporting the Commission's conclusion.[8]

In *NCAA*, we held that a "naked restraint on price and output requires some competitive justification even in the absence of a detailed market analysis." Elsewhere, we held that "no elaborate industry analysis is required to demonstrate the anticompetitive character of "horizontal agreements among competitors to refuse to discuss prices, *Engineers*, or to withhold a particular desired service, *Indiana Dentists* (quoting *Engineers*). In each of these cases, which have formed the basis for what has come to be called abbreviated or "quick-look" analysis under the rule of reason, an observer with even a rudimentary understanding of economics could conclude that the arrangements in question would have an anticompetitive effect on customers and markets. In *NCAA*, the league's television plan expressly limited output (the number of games that could be televised) and fixed a minimum price. In *Engineers*, the restraint was "an absolute ban on competitive bidding." In *Indiana Dentists*, the restraint was "a horizontal agreement among the participating dentists to withhold from their customers a particular service that they desire." As in such cases, quick-look analysis carries the day when the great likelihood of anticompetitive effects can easily be ascertained. . . .

The case before us, however, fails to present a situation in which the likelihood of anticompetitive effects is comparably obvious. Even on Justice Breyer's view that bars on truthful and verifiable price and quality advertising are prima facie anticompetitive, and place the burden of procompetitive justification on those who agree to adopt them, the very issue at the threshold of this case is whether professional price and quality advertising is sufficiently verifiable in theory and in fact to fall within such a general rule. Ultimately our disagreement with Justice Breyer turns on our different responses to this

---

[8] We leave to the Court of Appeals the question whether on remand it can effectively assess the Commission's decision for substantial evidence on the record, or whether it must remand to the Commission for a more extensive rule-of-reason analysis on the basis of an enhanced record.

¶221 *California Dental Association*

issue. Whereas he accepts, as the Ninth Circuit seems to have done, that the restrictions here were like restrictions on advertisement of price and quality generally, it seems to us that the CDA's advertising restrictions might plausibly be thought to have a net procompetitive effect, or possibly no effect at all on competition. The restrictions on both discount and nondiscount advertising are, at least on their face, designed to avoid false or deceptive advertising in a market characterized by striking disparities between the information available to the professional and the patient.[10] . . . In a market for professional services, in which advertising is relatively rare and the comparability of service packages not easily established, the difficulty for customers or potential competitors to get and verify information about the price and availability of services magnifies the dangers to competition associated with misleading advertising. What is more, the quality of professional services tends to resist either calibration or monitoring by individual patients or clients, partly because of the specialized knowledge required to evaluate the services, and partly because of the difficulty in determining whether, and the degree to which, an outcome is attributable to the quality of services (like a poor job of tooth-filling) or to something else (like a very tough walnut). . . . Patients' attachments to particular professionals, the rationality of which is difficult to assess, complicate the picture even further. . . . The existence of such significant challenges to informed decisionmaking by the customer for professional services immediately suggests that advertising restrictions arguably protecting patients from misleading or irrelevant advertising call for more than cursory treatment as obviously comparable to classic horizontal agreements to limit output or price competition.

The explanation proffered by the Court of Appeals for the likely anticompetitive effect of the CDA's restrictions on discount advertising began with the unexceptionable statements that "price advertising is fundamental to price competition," and that "[r]estrictions on the ability to advertise prices normally make it more difficult for consumers to find a lower price and for

---

[10] "The fact that a restraint operates upon a profession as distinguished from a business is, of course, relevant in determining whether that particular restraint violates the Sherman Act. It would be unrealistic to view the practice of professions as interchangeable with other business activities, and automatically to apply to the professions antitrust concepts which originated in other areas. The public service aspect, and other features of the professions, may require that a particular practice, which could properly be viewed as a violation of the Sherman Act in another context, be treated differently." Goldfarb v. Virginia State Bar, 421 U.S. 773, 788-789, n. 17.

California Dental Association ¶221

dentists to compete on the basis of price," (citing Bates v. State Bar of Ariz., 433 U.S. 350, 364 (1977); Morales v. Trans World Airlines, Inc., 504 U.S. 374, 388 (1992)). The court then acknowledged that, according to the CDA, the restrictions nonetheless furthered the "legitimate, indeed procompetitive, goal of preventing false and misleading price advertising." The Court of Appeals might, at this juncture, have recognized that the restrictions at issue here are very far from a total ban on price or discount advertising, and might have considered the possibility that the particular restrictions on professional advertising could have different effects from those "normally" found in the commercial world, even to the point of promoting competition by reducing the occurrence of unverifiable and misleading across-the-board discount advertising. Instead, the Court of Appeals confined itself to the brief assertion that the "CDA's disclosure requirements appear to prohibit across-the-board discounts because it is simply infeasible to disclose all of the information that is required," followed by the observation that "the record provides no evidence that the rule has in fact led to increased disclosure and transparency of dental pricing."

But these observations brush over the professional context and describe no anticompetitive effects. Assuming that the record in fact supports the conclusion that the CDA disclosure rules essentially bar advertisement of across-the-board discounts, it does not obviously follow that such a ban would have a net anticompetitive effect here. Whether advertisements that announced discounts for, say, first-time customers, would be less effective at conveying information relevant to competition if they listed the original and discounted prices for checkups, X-rays, and fillings, than they would be if they simply specified a percentage discount across the board, seems to us a question susceptible to empirical but not a priori analysis. In a suspicious world, the discipline of specific example may well be a necessary condition of plausibility for professional claims that for all practical purposes defy comparison shopping. It is also possible in principle that, even if across-the-board discount advertisements were more effective in drawing customers in the short run, the recurrence of some measure of intentional or accidental misstatement due to the breadth of their claims might leak out over time to make potential patients skeptical of any such across-the-board advertising, so undercutting the method's effectiveness. . . . It might be, too, that across-the-board discount advertisements would continue to attract business indefinitely, but might work precisely because they were misleading customers, and thus just because their effect would be anticompetitive, not procompetitive. Put another way, the CDA's rule appears to reflect the prediction that any costs to competition associated with the elimination of across-the-board advertising will be out-

9

¶221   California Dental Association

weighed by gains to consumer information (and hence competition) created by discount advertising that is exact, accurate, and more easily verifiable (at least by regulators). As a matter of economics this view may or may not be correct, but it is not implausible, and neither a court nor the Commission may initially dismiss it as presumptively wrong.[12]

In theory, it is true, the Court of Appeals neither ruled out the plausibility of some procompetitive support for the CDA's requirements nor foreclosed the utility of an evidentiary discussion on the point. The court indirectly acknowledged the plausibility of procompetitive justifications for the CDA's position when it stated that "the record provides no evidence that the rule has in fact led to increased disclosure and transparency of dental pricing." But because petitioner alone would have had the incentive to introduce such evidence, the statement sounds as though the Court of Appeals may have thought it was justified without further analysis to shift a burden to the CDA to adduce hard evidence of the procompetitive nature of its policy; the court's adversion to empirical evidence at the moment of this implicit burden-shifting underscores the leniency of its enquiry into evidence of the restrictions' anticompetitive effects.

The Court of Appeals was comparably tolerant in accepting the sufficiency of abbreviated rule-of-reason analysis as to the nonprice advertising restrictions. The court began with the argument that "[t]hese restrictions are in effect a form of output limitation, as they restrict the supply of information about individual dentists' services." . . . Although this sentence does indeed appear as cited, it is puzzling, given that the relevant output for antitrust purposes here is presumably not information or advertising, but dental services themselves. The question is not whether the universe of possible advertisements has been limited (as assuredly it has), but whether the limitation on advertisements obviously tends to limit the total delivery of dental services. The

---

[12] Justice Breyer suggests that our analysis is "of limited relevance" because "the basic question is whether this . . . theoretically redeeming virtue in fact offsets the restrictions' anticompetitive effects in this case." He thinks that the Commission and the Court of Appeals "adequately answered that question," but the absence of any empirical evidence on this point indicates that the question was not answered, merely avoided by the implicit burden-shifting of the kind accepted by Justice Breyer. The point is that before a theoretical claim of anticompetitive effects can justify shifting to a defendant the burden to show empirical evidence of procompetitive effects, as quick-look analysis in effect requires, there must be some indication that the court making the decision has properly identified the theoretical basis for the anticompetitive effects and considered whether the effects actually are anticompetitive. Where, as here, the circumstances of the restriction are somewhat complex, assumption alone will not do.

10

court came closest to addressing this latter question when it went on to assert that limiting advertisements regarding quality and safety "prevents dentists from fully describing the package of services they offer," adding that "[t]he restrictions may also affect output more directly, as quality and comfort advertising may induce some customers to obtain nonemergency care when they might not otherwise do so." This suggestion about output is also puzzling. If quality advertising actually induces some patients to obtain more care than they would in its absence, then restricting such advertising would reduce the demand for dental services, not the supply; and it is of course the producers' supply of a good in relation to demand that is normally relevant in determining whether a producer-imposed output limitation has the anticompetitive effect of artificially raising prices.[13]

Although the Court of Appeals acknowledged the CDA's view that "claims about quality are inherently unverifiable and therefore misleading," it responded that this concern "does not justify banning all quality claims without regard to whether they are, in fact, false or misleading." As a result, the court said, "the restriction is a sufficiently naked restraint on output to justify quick look analysis." The court assumed, in these words, that some dental quality claims may escape justifiable censure, because they are both verifiable and true. But its implicit assumption fails to explain why it gave no weight to the countervailing, and at least equally plausible, suggestion that restricting difficult-to-verify claims about quality or patient comfort would have a procompetitive effect by preventing misleading or false claims that distort the market. It is, indeed, entirely possible to understand the CDA's restrictions on unverifiable quality and comfort advertising as nothing more than a procompetitive ban on puffery, cf. *Bates*, 433 U.S., at 366 (claims relating to the quality of legal services "probably are not susceptible of precise measurement or verification and, under some circumstances, might well be deceptive or misleading to the public, or even false"); id., at 383-384 ("[A]dvertising claims as to the quality of services . . . are not susceptible of measurement or verification; accordingly, such claims may be so likely to be misleading as to

---

[13] Justice Breyer wonders if we "mea[n] this statement as an argument against the anticompetitive tendencies that flow from an agreement not to advertise service quality." But as the preceding sentence shows, we intend simply to question the logic of the Court of Appeals's suggestion that the restrictions are anticompetitive because they somehow "affect output," presumably with the intent to raise prices by limiting supply while demand remains constant. We do not mean to deny that an agreement not to advertise service quality might have anticompetitive effects. We merely mean that, absent further analysis of the kind Justice Breyer undertakes, it is not possible to conclude that the net effect of this particular restriction is anticompetitive.

¶221 *California Dental Association*

warrant restriction"), notwithstanding Justice Breyer's citation (to a Commission discussion that never faces the issue of the unverifiability of professional quality claims, raised in *Bates*).

The point is not that the CDA's restrictions necessarily have the procompetitive effect claimed by the CDA; it is possible that banning quality claims might have no effect at all on competitiveness if, for example, many dentists made very much the same sort of claims. And it is also of course possible that the restrictions might in the final analysis be anticompetitive. The point, rather, is that the plausibility of competing claims about the effects of the professional advertising restrictions rules out the indulgently abbreviated review to which the Commission's order was treated. The obvious anticompetitive effect that triggers abbreviated analysis has not been shown.

In light of our focus on the adequacy of the Court of Appeals's analysis, Justice Breyer's thorough-going, de novo antitrust analysis contains much to impress on its own merits but little to demonstrate the sufficiency of the Court of Appeals's review. The obligation to give a more deliberate look than a quick one does not arise at the door of this Court and should not be satisfied here in the first instance. Had the Court of Appeals engaged in a painstaking discussion in a league with Justice Breyer's (compare his 14 pages with the Ninth Circuit's 8), and had it confronted the comparability of these restrictions to bars on clearly verifiable advertising, its reasoning might have sufficed to justify its conclusion. Certainly Justice Breyer's treatment of the antitrust issues here is no "quick look." Lingering is more like it, and indeed Justice Breyer, not surprisingly, stops short of endorsing the Court of Appeals's discussion as adequate to the task at hand.

Saying here that the Court of Appeals's conclusion at least required a more extended examination of the possible factual underpinnings than it received is not, of course, necessarily to call for the fullest market analysis. Although we have said that a challenge to a "naked restraint on price and output" need not be supported by "a detailed market analysis" in order to "requir[e] some competitive justification," *NCAA*, it does not follow that every case attacking a less obviously anticompetitive restraint (like this one) is a candidate for plenary market examination. The truth is that our categories of analysis of anticompetitive effect are less fixed than terms like "per se," "quick look," and "rule of reason" tend to make them appear. We have recognized, for example, that "there is often no bright line separating per se from Rule of Reason analysis," since "considerable inquiry into market conditions" may be required before the application of any so-called "per se" condemnation is justified. Id. "[W]hether the ultimate finding is the product of a presumption

12

California Dental Association ¶221

or actual market analysis, the essential inquiry remains the same—whether or not the challenged restraint enhances competition." Id. Indeed, the scholar who enriched antitrust law with the metaphor of "the twinkling of an eye" for the most condensed rule-of-reason analysis himself cautioned against the risk of misleading even in speaking of a 'spectrum' of adequate reasonableness analysis for passing upon antitrust claims: "There is always something of a sliding scale in appraising reasonableness, but the sliding scale formula deceptively suggests greater precision than we can hope for . . . . Nevertheless, the quality of proof required should vary with the circumstances." P. Areeda, Antitrust Law ¶1507, p. 402 (1986). At the same time, Professor Areeda also emphasized the necessity, particularly great in the quasi-common law realm of antitrust, that courts explain the logic of their conclusions. "By exposing their reasoning, judges . . . are subjected to others' critical analyses, which in turn can lead to better understanding for the future." Id., ¶1500, at 364. As the circumstances here demonstrate, there is generally no categorical line to be drawn between restraints that give rise to an intuitively obvious inference of anticompetitive effect and those that call for more detailed treatment. What is required, rather, is an enquiry meet for the case, looking to the circumstances, details, and logic of a restraint. The object is to see whether the experience of the market has been so clear, or necessarily will be, that a confident conclusion about the principal tendency of a restriction will follow from a quick (or at least quicker) look, in place of a more sedulous one. And of course what we see may vary over time, if rule-of-reason analyses in case after case reach identical conclusions. For now, at least, a less quick look was required for the initial assessment of the tendency of these professional advertising restrictions. Because the Court of Appeals did not scrutinize the assumption of relative anticompetitive tendencies, we vacate the judgment and remand the case for a fuller consideration of the issue. It is so ordered.

Justice BREYER, with whom Justice STEVENS, Justice KENNEDY, and Justice GINSBURG join, concurring in part and dissenting in part. I agree with the Court that the Federal Trade Commission has jurisdiction over petitioner, and I join Parts I and II of its opinion. I also agree that in a "rule of reason" antitrust case "the quality of proof required should vary with the circumstances," that "[w]hat is required . . . is an enquiry meet for the case," and that the object is a "confident conclusion about the principal tendency of a restriction." But I do not agree that the Court has properly applied those unobjectionable principles here. In my view, a traditional application of the rule of reason to the facts as found by the Commission requires affirming the Commission—just as the Court of Appeals did below.

I

The Commission's conclusion is lawful if its "factual findings," insofar as they are supported by "substantial evidence," "make out a violation of Sherman Act §1." *Indiana Dentists*. To determine whether that is so, I would not simply ask whether the restraints at issue are anticompetitive overall. Rather, like the Court of Appeals (and the Commission), I would break that question down into four classical, subsidiary antitrust questions: (1) What is the specific restraint at issue? (2) What are its likely anticompetitive effects? (3) Are there offsetting procompetitive justifications? (4) Do the parties have sufficient market power to make a difference?

A

The most important question is the first: What are the specific restraints at issue? See, e.g., *NCAA*; *BMI*. Those restraints do not include merely the agreement to which the California Dental Association's (Dental Association or Association) ethical rule literally refers, namely, a promise to refrain from advertising that is "'false or misleading in any material respect.'" Instead, the Commission found a set of restraints arising out of the way the Dental Association implemented this innocent-sounding ethical rule in practice, through advisory opinions, guidelines, enforcement policies, and review of membership applications. As implemented, the ethical rule reached beyond its nominal target, to prevent truthful and nondeceptive advertising. In particular, the Commission determined that the rule, in practice:

> (1) "precluded advertising that characterized a dentist's fees as being low, reasonable, or affordable,"
> (2) "precluded advertising . . . of across the board discounts," and
> (3) "prohibit[ed] all quality claims."

Whether the Dental Association's basic rule as implemented actually restrained the truthful and nondeceptive advertising of low prices, across-the-board discounts, and quality service are questions of fact. The Administrative Law Judge (ALJ) and the Commission may have found those questions difficult ones. But both the ALJ and the Commission ultimately found against the Dental Association in respect to these facts. And the question for us—whether those agency findings are supported by substantial evidence, see *Indiana Dentists*—is not difficult.

California Dental Association

The Court of Appeals referred explicitly to some of the evidence that it found adequate to support the Commission's conclusions. It pointed out, for example, that the Dental Association's "advisory opinions and guidelines indicate that . . . descriptions of prices as 'reasonable' or 'low' do not comply" with the Association's rule; that in "numerous cases" the Association "advised members of objections to special offers, senior citizen discounts, and new patient discounts, apparently without regard to their truth"; and that one advisory opinion "expressly states that claims as to the quality of services are inherently likely to be false or misleading," all "without any particular consideration of whether" such statements were "true or false."

The Commission itself had before it far more evidence. It referred to instances in which the Association, without regard for the truthfulness of the statements at issue, recommended denial of membership to dentists wishing to advertise, for example, "reasonable fees quoted in advance," "major savings," or "making teeth cleaning . . . inexpensive." It referred to testimony that "across-the-board discount advertising in literal compliance with the requirements 'would probably take two pages in the telephone book' and '[n]obody is going to really advertise in that fashion.'" And it pointed to many instances in which the Dental Association suppressed such advertising claims as "we guarantee all dental work for 1 year," "latest in cosmetic dentistry," and "gentle dentistry in a caring environment."

I need not review the evidence further, for this Court has said that "substantial evidence" is a matter for the courts of appeals, and that it "will intervene only in what ought to be the rare instance when the standard appears to have been misapprehended or grossly misapplied." Universal Camera Corp. v. NLRB, 340 U.S. 474, 490-491 (1951). I have said enough to make clear that this is not a case warranting our intervention. Consequently, we must decide only the basic legal question whether the three restraints described above unreasonably restrict competition.

B

Do each of the three restrictions mentioned have "the potential for genuine adverse effects on competition"? *Indiana Dentists*; 7 P. Areeda, Antitrust Law ¶1503a, pp. 372-377 (1986) (hereinafter Areeda). I should have thought that the anticompetitive tendencies of the three restrictions were obvious. An agreement not to advertise that a fee is reasonable, that service is inexpensive, or that a customer will receive a discount makes it more difficult for a dentist to inform customers that he charges a lower price. If the customer does not know about a lower price, he will find it more difficult to buy lower price service. That fact, in turn, makes it less likely that a dentist will obtain more customers by offering lower prices. And that likelihood means that dentists will prove less likely to offer lower prices. But why should I have to spell out the obvious? To restrain truthful advertising about lower prices is likely to restrict competition in respect to price—"the central nervous system of the economy." *Socony*; cf., e.g., Bates v. State Bar of Ariz., 433 U.S. 350, 364 (1977) (price advertising plays an "indispensable role in the allocation of resources in a free enterprise system"); Virginia Bd. of Pharmacy v. Virginia Citizens Consumer Council, Inc., 425 U.S. 748, 765 (1976). The Commission thought this fact sufficient to hold (in the alternative) that the price advertising restrictions were unlawful per se. . . . For present purposes, I need not decide whether the Commission was right in applying a per se rule. I need only assume a rule of reason applies, and note the serious anticompetitive tendencies of the price advertising restraints.

The restrictions on the advertising of service quality also have serious anticompetitive tendencies. This is not a case of "mere puffing," as the FTC recognized. The days of my youth, when the billboards near Emeryville, California, home of AAA baseball's Oakland Oaks, displayed the name of "Painless" Parker, Dentist, are long gone—along with the Oakland Oaks. But some parents may still want to know that a particular dentist makes a point of "gentle care." Others may want to know about 1-year dental work guarantees. To restrict that kind of service quality advertisement is to restrict competition over the quality of service itself, for, unless consumers know, they may not purchase, and dentists may not compete to supply that which will make little difference to the demand for their services. That, at any rate, is the theory of the Sherman Act. And it is rather late in the day for anyone to deny the significant anticompetitive tendencies of an agreement that restricts competition in any legitimate respect, see, e.g., Paramount Famous Lasky Corp. v. United States, 282 U.S. 30, 43 (1930); United States v. First Nat. Pictures, Inc., 282 U.S. 44, 54-55 (1930), let alone one that inhibits customers from learning about the quality of a dentist's service.

Nor did the Commission rely solely on the unobjectionable proposition that a restriction on the ability of dentists to advertise on quality is likely to limit their incentive to compete on quality. Rather, the Commission pointed to record evidence affirmatively establishing that quality-based competition is important to dental consumers in California. Unsurprisingly, these consumers choose dental services based at least in part on "information about the type and quality of service." Similarly, as the Commission noted, the ALJ credited testimony to the effect that "advertising the comfort of services will 'abso-

California Dental Association ¶221

lutely' bring in more patients," and, conversely, that restraining the ability to advertise based on quality would decrease the number of patients that a dentist could attract. Finally, the Commission looked to the testimony of dentists who themselves had suffered adverse effects on their business when forced by petitioner to discontinue advertising quality of care.

The FTC found that the price advertising restrictions amounted to a "naked attempt to eliminate price competition." It found that the service quality advertising restrictions "deprive consumers of information they value and of healthy competition for their patronage." It added that the "anticompetitive nature of these restrictions" was "plain." The Court of Appeals agreed. I do not believe it possible to deny the anticompetitive tendencies I have mentioned.

C

We must also ask whether, despite their anticompetitive tendencies, these restrictions might be justified by other procompetitive tendencies or redeeming virtues. See 7 Areeda, ¶1504, at 377-383. This is a closer question—at least in theory. The Dental Association argues that the three relevant restrictions are inextricably tied to a legitimate Association effort to restrict false or misleading advertising. The Association, the argument goes, had to prevent dentists from engaging in the kind of truthful, nondeceptive advertising that it banned in order effectively to stop dentists from making unverifiable claims about price or service quality, which claims would mislead the consumer.

The problem with this or any similar argument is an empirical one. Notwithstanding its theoretical plausibility, the record does not bear out such a claim. The Commission, which is expert in the area of false and misleading advertising, was uncertain whether petitioner had even made the claim. It characterized petitioner's efficiencies argument as rooted in the (unproved) factual assertion that its ethical rule "challenges only advertising that is false or misleading." Regardless, the Court of Appeals wrote, in respect to the price restrictions, that "the record provides no evidence that the rule has in fact led to increased disclosure and transparency of dental pricing." With respect to quality advertising, the Commission stressed that the Association "offered no convincing argument, let alone evidence, that consumers of dental services have been, or are likely to be, harmed by the broad categories of advertising it restricts." Nor did the Court of Appeals think that the Association's unsubstantiated contention that "claims about quality are inherently unverifiable and therefore misleading" could "justify banning all quality claims without regard to whether they are, in fact, false or misleading."

17

¶221 *California Dental Association*

With one exception, my own review of the record reveals no significant evidentiary support for the proposition that the Association's members must agree to ban truthful price and quality advertising in order to stop untruthful claims. The one exception is the obvious fact that one can stop untruthful advertising if one prohibits all advertising. But since the Association made virtually no effort to sift the false from the true, that fact does not make out a valid antitrust defense. See *NCAA*; 7 Areeda, ¶1505, at 383-384.

In the usual Sherman Act §1 case, the defendant bears the burden of establishing a procompetitive justification. See *Engineers*. . . . And the Court of Appeals was correct when it concluded that no such justification had been established here.

version of a per se rule – but defeasible

D

I shall assume that the Commission must prove one additional circumstance, namely, that the Association's restraints would likely have made a real difference in the marketplace. See 7 Areeda, ¶1503, at 376-377. The Commission, disagreeing with the ALJ on this single point, found that the Association did possess enough market power to make a difference. In at least one region of California, the mid-Peninsula, its members accounted for more than 90% of the marketplace; on average they accounted for 75%. In addition, entry by new dentists into the market place is fairly difficult. Dental education is expensive (leaving graduates of dental school with $50,000-$100,000 of debt), as is opening a new dentistry office (which costs $75,000-$100,000). And Dental Association members believe membership in the Association is important, valuable, and recognized as such by the public.

These facts, in the Court of Appeals' view, were sufficient to show "enough market power to harm competition through [the Association's] standard setting in the area of advertising." And that conclusion is correct. Restrictions on advertising price discounts in Palo Alto may make a difference because potential patients may not respond readily to discount advertising by the handful (10%) of dentists who are not members of the Association. And that fact, in turn, means that the remaining 90% will prove less likely to engage in price competition. Facts such as these have previously led this Court to find market power—unless the defendant has overcome the showing with strong contrary evidence. See, e.g., *Indiana Dentists*; cf. *United States v. Loew's Inc.*, 371 U.S. 38, 45 (1962); *Brown Shoe*; accord, *Alcoa*. I can find no reason for departing from that precedent here.

II

In the Court's view, the legal analysis conducted by the Court of Appeals was insufficient, and the Court remands the case for a more thorough application of the rule of reason. But in what way did the Court of Appeals fail? I find the Court's answers to this question unsatisfactory—when one divides the overall Sherman Act question into its traditional component parts and adheres to traditional judicial practice for allocating the burdens of persuasion in an antitrust case.

Did the Court of Appeals misconceive the anticompetitive tendencies of the restrictions? After all, the object of the rule of reason is to separate those restraints that "may suppress or even destroy competition" from those that "merely regulat[e] and perhaps thereby promot[e] competition." *Chicago Board of Trade*. The majority says that the Association's "advertising restrictions might plausibly be thought to have a net procompetitive effect, or possibly no effect at all on competition." It adds that

> "advertising restrictions arguably protecting patients from misleading or irrelevant advertising call for more than cursory treatment as obviously comparable to classic horizontal agreements to limit output or price competition."

And it criticizes the Court of Appeals for failing to recognize that "the restrictions at issue here are very far from a total ban on price or discount advertising" and that "the particular restrictions on professional advertising could have different effects from those 'normally' found in the commercial world, even to the point of promoting competition . . . ."

The problem with these statements is that the Court of Appeals did consider the relevant differences. It rejected the legal "treatment" customarily applied "to classic horizontal agreements to limit output or price competition"—i.e., the FTC's (alternative) per se approach. It did so because the Association's "policies do not, on their face, ban truthful nondeceptive ads"; instead, they "have been enforced in a way that restricts truthful advertising." It added that "[t]he value of restricting false advertising . . . counsels some caution in attacking rules that purport to do so but merely sweep too broadly."

Did the Court of Appeals misunderstand the nature of an anticompetitive effect? The Court says:

> "If quality advertising actually induces some patients to obtain more care than they would in its absence, then restricting such advertising would reduce the

demand for dental services, not the supply; and . . . the producers' supply . . . is normally relevant in determining whether a . . . limitation has the anticompetitive effect of artificially raising prices."

But if the Court means this statement as an argument against the anticompetitive tendencies that flow from an agreement not to advertise service quality, I believe it is the majority, and not the Court of Appeals, that is mistaken. An agreement not to advertise, say, "gentle care" is anticompetitive because it imposes an artificial barrier against each dentist's independent decision to advertise gentle care. That barrier, in turn, tends to inhibit those dentists who want to supply gentle care from getting together with those customers who want to buy gentle care. . . . There is adequate reason to believe that tendency present in this case.

Did the Court of Appeals inadequately consider possible procompetitive justifications? The Court seems to think so, for it says:

"[T]he [Association's] rule appears to reflect the prediction that any costs to competition associated with the elimination of across-the-board advertising will be outweighed by gains to consumer information (and hence competition) created by discount advertising that is exact, accurate, and more easily verifiable (at least by regulators)."

That may or may not be an accurate assessment of the Association's motives in adopting its rule, but it is of limited relevance. Cf. *Chicago Board of Trade*. The basic question is whether this, or some other, theoretically redeeming virtue in fact offsets the restrictions' anticompetitive effects in this case. Both court and Commission adequately answered that question.

The Commission found that the defendant did not make the necessary showing that a redeeming virtue existed in practice. The Court of Appeals, asking whether the rules, as enforced, "augment[ed] competition and increase[d] market efficiency," found the Commission's conclusion supported by substantial evidence. That is why the court said that "the record provides no evidence that the rule has in fact led to increased disclosure and transparency of dental pricing"—which is to say that the record provides no evidence that the effects, though anticompetitive, are nonetheless redeemed or justified.

The majority correctly points out that "petitioner alone would have had the incentive to introduce such evidence" of procompetitive justification. (Indeed, that is one of the reasons defendants normally bear the burden of persuasion about redeeming virtues.) But despite this incentive, petitioner's brief in this Court offers nothing concrete to counter the Commission's conclusion that the record does not support the claim of justification. Petitioner's failure to produce such evidence itself "explain[s] why [the lower court] gave no weight to the . . . suggestion that restricting difficult-to-verify claims about quality or patient comfort would have a procompetitive effect by preventing misleading or false claims that distort the market."

With respect to the restraint on advertising across-the-board discounts, the majority summarizes its concerns as follows: "Assuming that the record in fact supports the conclusion that the [Association's] disclosure rules essentially bar advertisement of [such] discounts, it does not obviously follow that such a ban would have a net anticompetitive effect here." I accept, rather than assume, the premise: The FTC found that the disclosure rules did bar advertisement of across-the-board discounts, and that finding is supported by substantial evidence. And I accept as literally true the conclusion that the Court says follows from that premise, namely, that "net anticompetitive effects" do not "obviously" follow from that premise. But obviousness is not the point. With respect to any of the three restraints found by the Commission, whether "net anticompetitive effects" follow is a matter of how the Commission, and, here, the Court of Appeals, have answered the questions I laid out at the beginning. Has the Commission shown that the restriction has anticompetitive tendencies? It has. Has the Association nonetheless shown offsetting virtues? It has not. Has the Commission shown market power sufficient for it to believe that the restrictions will likely make a real world difference? It has.

The upshot, in my view, is that the Court of Appeals, applying ordinary antitrust principles, reached an unexceptional conclusion. It is the same legal conclusion that this Court itself reached in *Indiana Dentists*—a much closer case than this one. There the Court found that an agreement by dentists not to submit dental X rays to insurers violated the rule of reason. The anticompetitive tendency of that agreement was to reduce competition among dentists in respect to their willingness to submit X rays to insurers—a matter in respect to which consumers are relatively indifferent, as compared to advertising of price discounts and service quality, the matters at issue here. The redeeming virtue in *Indiana Dentists* was the alleged undesirability of having insurers consider a range of matters when deciding whether treatment was justified—a virtue no less plausible, and no less proved, than the virtue offered here. The "power" of the dentists to enforce their agreement was no greater than that at issue here (control of 75% to 90% of the relevant markets). It is difficult to see how the two cases can be reconciled. . . .

For these reasons, I respectfully dissent from Part III of the Court's opinion.

¶222												*Competition Collaboration Guidelines*

Page 248. After ¶222, add the following:

222'. Determining Which Restraints Are Reasonable. In 2000, the Federal Trade Commission and the Department of Justice jointly issued the Antitrust Guidelines for Collaborations Among Competitors. The Competitor Collaboration Guidelines describe general principles for evaluating horizontal agreements that may restrict competition among the collaborators, present an analytical framework for assessing such agreements (focusing especially on analysis under the rule of reason), and describe antitrust safety zones (mainly, for collaborations whose participants account for no more than twenty percent of the market), within which the agencies will not challenge agreements in the absence of extraordinary circumstances. Throughout, there are examples that are described and analyzed, to illustrate how the Guidelines would be applied. These Guidelines are reproduced in an Appendix to this Supplement.

2E. Concerted Refusals to Deal

Page 365. After ¶266, add the following:

NYNEX v. DISCON
119 S. Ct. 493 (1998)

Justice BREYER. In this case we ask whether the antitrust rule that group boycotts are illegal per se as set forth in *Klor's,* applies to a buyer's decision to buy from one seller rather than another, when that decision cannot be justified in terms of ordinary competitive objectives. We hold that the per se group boycott rule does not apply.

I

Before 1984 American Telephone and Telegraph Company (AT&T) supplied most of the Nation's telephone service and, through wholly owned subsidiaries such as Western Electric, it also supplied much of the Nation's telephone equipment. In 1984 an antitrust consent decree took AT&T out of the local telephone service business and left AT&T a long-distance telephone service provider, competing with such firms as MCI and Sprint. . . . The decree transformed AT&T's formerly owned local telephone companies into independent firms. At the same time, the decree insisted that those local firms help assure competitive long-distance service by guaranteeing long-distance companies physical access to their systems and to their local customers. . . . To guarantee that physical access, some local telephone firms had to install new call-switching equipment; and to install new call-switching equipment, they often had to remove old call-switching equipment. This case involves the business of removing that old switching equipment (and other obsolete telephone equipment)—a business called "removal services."

Discon, Inc., the respondent, sold removal services used by New York Telephone Company, a firm supplying local telephone service in much of New York State and parts of Connecticut. New York Telephone is a subsidiary of NYNEX Corporation. NYNEX also owns Materiel Enterprises Company, a purchasing entity that bought removal services for New York Telephone. Discon, in a lengthy detailed complaint, alleged that the NYNEX defendants (namely, NYNEX, New York Telephone, Materiel Enterprises, and several NYNEX related individuals) engaged in unfair, improper, and anticompetitive activities in order to hurt Discon and to benefit Discon's

23

removal services competitor, AT&T Technologies, a lineal descendant of Western Electric. The Federal District Court dismissed Discon's complaint for failure to state a claim. The Court of Appeals for the Second Circuit affirmed that dismissal with an exception, and that exception is before us for consideration.

The Second Circuit focused on one of Discon's specific claims, a claim that Materiel Enterprises had switched its purchases from Discon to Discon's competitor, AT&T Technologies, as part of an attempt to defraud local telephone service customers by hoodwinking regulators. According to Discon, Materiel Enterprises would pay AT&T Technologies more than Discon would have charged for similar removal services. It did so because it could pass the higher prices on to New York Telephone, which in turn could pass those prices on to telephone consumers in the form of higher regulatory-agency-approved telephone service charges. At the end of the year, Materiel Enterprises would receive a special rebate from AT&T Technologies, which Materiel Enterprises would share with its parent, NYNEX. Discon added that it refused to participate in this fraudulent scheme, with the result that Materiel Enterprises would not buy from Discon, and Discon went out of business.

These allegations, the Second Circuit said, state a cause of action under §1 of the Sherman Act, though under a "different legal theory" from the one articulated by Discon. The Second Circuit conceded that ordinarily "the decision to discriminate in favor of one supplier over another will have a pro-competitive intent and effect." But, it added, in this case, "no such pro-competitive rationale appears on the face of the complaint." Rather, the complaint alleges Materiel Enterprises' decision to buy from AT&T Technologies, rather than from Discon, was intended to be, and was, "anti-competitive." Hence, "Discon has alleged a cause of action under, at least, the rule of reason, and possibly under the per se rule applied to group boycotts in Klor's, if the restraint of trade 'has no purpose except stifling competition.'".
. . . For somewhat similar reasons the Second Circuit believed the complaint stated a valid claim of conspiracy to monopolize under §2 of the Sherman Act.

The Second Circuit noted that the Courts of Appeals are uncertain as to whether, or when, the per se group boycott rule applies to a decision by a purchaser to favor one supplier over another (which the Second Circuit called a "two-firm group boycott"). We granted certiorari in order to consider the applicability of the per se group boycott rule where a single buyer favors one seller over another, albeit for an improper reason.

II

As this Court has made clear, the Sherman Act's prohibition of "[e]very" agreement in "restraint of trade" prohibits only agreements that unreasonably restrain trade.... Yet certain kinds of agreements will so often prove so harmful to competition and so rarely prove justified that the antitrust laws do not require proof that an agreement of that kind is, in fact, anticompetitive in the particular circumstances.... An agreement of such a kind is unlawful per se....

The Court has found the per se rule applicable in certain group boycott cases.... The case before us involves *Klor's*. The Second Circuit did not forbid the defendants to introduce evidence of "justification." To the contrary, it invited the defendants to do so, for it said that the "per se rule" would apply only if no "pro-competitive justification" were to be found. Cf. 7 P. Areeda & H. Hovenkamp, Antitrust Law ¶1510, p. 416 (1986) ("Boycotts are said to be unlawful per se but justifications are routinely considered in defining the forbidden category"). Thus, the specific legal question before us is whether an antitrust court considering an agreement by a buyer to purchase goods or services from one supplier rather than another should (after examining the buyer's reasons or justifications) apply the per se rule if it finds no legitimate business reason for that purchasing decision. We conclude no boycott-related per se rule applies and that the plaintiff here must allege and prove harm, not just to a single competitor, but to the competitive process, i.e., to competition itself.

Our conclusion rests in large part upon precedent, for precedent limits the per se rule in the boycott context to cases involving horizontal agreements among direct competitors. The agreement in *FOGA* involved what may be called a group boycott in the strongest sense: A group of competitors threatened to withhold business from third parties unless those third parties would help them injure their directly competing rivals. Although *Klor's* involved a threat made by a single powerful firm, it also involved a horizontal agreement among those threatened, namely, the appliance suppliers, to hurt a competitor of the retailer who made the threat. See also P. Areeda & L. Kaplow, Antitrust Analysis: Problems, Text, Cases 333 (5th ed. 1997) (defining paradigmatic boycott as "collective action among a group of competitors that may inhibit the competitive vitality of rivals"); 11 H. Hovenkamp, Antitrust Law ¶1901e, pp. 189-190 (1998). This Court emphasized in *Klor's* that the agreement at issue was "not a case of a single trader refusing to deal with another, nor even of a manufacturer and a dealer agreeing to an exclusive distributorship. Alleged in this complaint is a wide combination consisting of manufacturers, distributors and a retailer."

This Court subsequently pointed out specifically that *Klor's* was a case involving not simply a "vertical" agreement between supplier and customer, but a case that also involved a "horizontal" agreement among competitors. See *Business Electronics*. And in doing so, the Court held that a "vertical restraint is not illegal per se unless it includes some agreement on price or price levels." This precedent makes the per se rule inapplicable, for the case before us concerns only a vertical agreement and a vertical restraint, a restraint that takes the form of depriving a supplier of a potential customer. See 11 Hovenkamp, supra, ¶ 1902d, at 198.

Nor have we found any special feature of this case that could distinguish it from the precedent we have just discussed. We concede Discon's claim that the petitioners' behavior hurt consumers by raising telephone service rates. But that consumer injury naturally flowed not so much from a less competitive market for removal services, as from the exercise of market power that is lawfully in the hands of a monopolist, namely, New York Telephone, combined with a deception worked upon the regulatory agency that prevented the agency from controlling New York Telephone's exercise of its monopoly power.

To apply the per se rule here—where the buyer's decision, though not made for competitive reasons, composes part of a regulatory fraud—would transform cases involving business behavior that is improper for various reasons, say, cases involving nepotism or personal pique, into treble-damages antitrust cases. And that per se rule would discourage firms from changing suppliers—even where the competitive process itself does not suffer harm. Cf. Poller v. Columbia Broadcasting System, 368 U.S. 464, 484 (1962) (Harlan, J., dissenting) (citing *Packard*).

The freedom to switch suppliers lies close to the heart of the competitive process that the antitrust laws seek to encourage. . . . At the same time, other laws, for example, "unfair competition" laws, business tort laws, or regulatory laws, provide remedies for various "competitive practices thought to be offensive to proper standards of business morality." 3 P. Areeda & H. Hovenkamp, Antitrust Law ¶ 651d, p. 78 (1996). Thus, this Court has refused to apply per se reasoning in cases involving that kind of activity. See *Brooke Group* ("Even an act of pure malice by one business competitor against another does not, without more, state a claim under the federal antitrust laws"). . . .

Discon points to another special feature of its complaint, namely, its claim that Materiel Enterprises hoped to drive Discon from the market lest Discon reveal its behavior to New York Telephone or to the relevant regulatory agency. That hope, says Discon, amounts to a special anticompetitive motive.

We do not see how the presence of this special motive, however, could make a significant difference. That motive does not turn Materiel Enterprises' actions into a "boycott" within the meaning of this Court's precedents. Nor, for that matter, do we understand how Discon believes the motive affected Materiel Enterprises' behavior. Why would Discon's demise have made Discon's employees less likely, rather than more likely, to report the overcharge/rebate scheme to telephone regulators? Regardless, a per se rule that would turn upon a showing that a defendant not only knew about but also hoped for a firm's demise would create a legal distinction—between corporate knowledge and corporate motive—that does not necessarily correspond to behavioral differences and which would be difficult to prove, making the resolution of already complex antitrust cases yet more difficult. We cannot find a convincing reason why the presence of this special motive should lead to the application of the per se rule.

Finally, we shall consider an argument that is related tangentially to Discon's per se claims. The complaint alleges that New York Telephone (through Materiel Enterprises) was the largest buyer of removal services in New York State and that only AT&T Technologies competed for New York Telephone's business. One might ask whether these accompanying allegations are sufficient to warrant application of a *Klor's*-type presumption of consequent harm to the competitive process itself.

We believe that these allegations do not do so, for, as we have said, antitrust law does not permit the application of the per se rule in the boycott context in the absence of a horizontal agreement. (Though in other contexts, say, vertical price fixing, conduct may fall within the scope of a per se rule not at issue here. See, e.g., *Dr. Miles*.) The complaint itself explains why any such presumption would be particularly inappropriate here, for it suggests the presence of other potential or actual competitors, which fact, in the circumstances, could argue against the likelihood of anticompetitive harm. The complaint says, for example, that New York Telephone itself was a potential competitor in that New York Telephone considered removing its equipment by itself, and in fact did perform a few jobs itself. The complaint also suggests that other nearby small local telephone companies needing removal services must have worked out some way to supply them. The complaint's description of the removal business suggests that entry was easy, perhaps to the point where other firms, employing workers who knew how to remove a switch and sell it for scrap, might have entered that business almost at will. To that extent, the complaint suggests other actual or potential competitors might have provided roughly similar checks upon "equipment removal" prices and services with or without Discon. At the least, the complaint provides no sound basis for assuming the contrary. Its simple allegation of harm to Discon does not automatically show injury to competition.

III

The Court of Appeals also upheld the complaint's charge of a conspiracy to monopolize in violation of §2 of the Sherman Act. It did so, however, on the understanding that the conspiracy in question consisted of the very same purchasing practices that we have previously discussed. Unless those agreements harmed the competitive process, they did not amount to a conspiracy to monopolize. We do not see, on the basis of the facts alleged, how Discon could succeed on this claim without prevailing on its §1 claim. . . . Given our conclusion that Discon has not alleged a §1 per se violation, we think it prudent to vacate this portion of the Court of Appeals' decision and allow the court to reconsider its finding of a §2 claim. . . .*

---

* On remand, the Court of Appeals remanded the case to the District Court to determine whether Discon's complaint stated a claim under the Supreme Court's requirement that a plaintiff demonstrate harm to the competitive process, that is, to competition itself. 184 F.3d 111 (2d Cir. 1999). The District Court ruled that it did not and dismissed the complaint. 86 F. Supp. 2d 154 (W.D.N.Y. 2000).

Chapter 3

Monopoly

3A. Monopolization

Page 476. After ¶312, add the following:

312'. Microsoft Litigation. The district court's conclusions of law in *Microsoft* are reproduced below. (The court's findings of fact are too lengthy to reproduce and are referenced in some detail in the conclusions of law. Interested readers can locate these findings at 84 F. Supp. 2d 9 (1999), http://www.microsoft.com/presspass/trial/c-fof/fof.asp, and http://www.usdoj. gov/atr/cases/f3800/msjudgex.htm.) This opinion covers not only the subject of monopolization, but also issues involving monopoly power (Chapter 3B), attempted monopolization (Chapter 3C), tying (Chapter 4B), and exclusive dealing (Chapter 4C). The opinion might be studied as a whole in the present chapter or at some later point, or each of its components can be examined in connection with the corresponding chapter.

The court's opinion is followed by its final judgment with regard to remedies. It is likely that there will be further developments after this Supplement has gone to press, involving appeal of the district court's decision as well as possible proceedings concerning relief. Future events can be followed on Microsoft's Web site, http://www.microsoft.com/presspass/trial/default.asp, and the Department of Justice's, http://www.usdoj.gov/atr/cases/ms _index.htm. Both sites already include court orders, briefs, affidavits, and other information regarding all phases of the litigation.

UNITED STATES v. MICROSOFT CORP.
87 F. Supp. 2d 30 (2000)

Judge JACKSON. The United States, nineteen individual states, and the District of Columbia ("the plaintiffs") bring these consolidated civil enforce-

¶312

ment actions against defendant Microsoft Corporation ("Microsoft") under the Sherman Antitrust Act. The plaintiffs charge, in essence, that Microsoft has waged an unlawful campaign in defense of its monopoly position in the market for operating systems designed to run on Intel-compatible personal computers ("PCs"). Specifically, the plaintiffs contend that Microsoft violated §2 of the Sherman Act by engaging in a series of exclusionary, anticompetitive, and predatory acts to maintain its monopoly power. They also assert that Microsoft attempted, albeit unsuccessfully to date, to monopolize the Web browser market, likewise in violation of §2. Finally, they contend that certain steps taken by Microsoft as part of its campaign to protect its monopoly power, namely tying its browser to its operating system and entering into exclusive dealing arrangements, violated §1 of the Act.

Upon consideration of the Court's Findings of Fact ("Findings"), filed herein on November 5, 1999, as amended on December 21, 1999, the proposed conclusions of law submitted by the parties, the briefs of amici curiae, and the argument of counsel thereon, the Court concludes that Microsoft maintained its monopoly power by anticompetitive means and attempted to monopolize the Web browser market, both in violation of §2. Microsoft also violated §1 of the Sherman Act by unlawfully tying its Web browser to its operating system. The facts found do not support the conclusion, however, that the effect of Microsoft's marketing arrangements with other companies constituted unlawful exclusive dealing under criteria established by leading decisions under §1.

The nineteen states and the District of Columbia ("the plaintiff states") seek to ground liability additionally under their respective antitrust laws. The Court is persuaded that the evidence in the record proving violations of the Sherman Act also satisfies the elements of analogous causes of action arising under the laws of each plaintiff state. For this reason, and for others stated below, the Court holds Microsoft liable under those particular state laws as well.

I. SECTION TWO OF THE SHERMAN ACT

    A. Maintenance of Monopoly Power by Anticompetitive Means . . .

        1. Monopoly Power . . .

In this case, the plaintiffs postulated the relevant market as being the worldwide licensing of Intel-compatible PC operating systems. Whether this

Microsoft Corp. ¶312

zone of commercial activity actually qualifies as a market, "monopolization of which may be illegal," depends on whether it includes all products "reasonably interchangeable by consumers for the same purposes." *Cellophane.* . . .

The Court has already found, based on the evidence in this record, that there are currently no products—and that there are not likely to be any in the near future—that a significant percentage of computer users worldwide could substitute for Intel-compatible PC operating systems without incurring substantial costs. Findings ¶¶18-29. The Court has further found that no firm not currently marketing Intel-compatible PC operating systems could start doing so in a way that would, within a reasonably short period of time, present a significant percentage of such consumers with a viable alternative to existing Intel-compatible PC operating systems. Id. ¶¶18, 30-32. From these facts, the Court has inferred that if a single firm or cartel controlled the licensing of all Intel-compatible PC operating systems worldwide, it could set the price of a license substantially above that which would be charged in a competitive market—and leave the price there for a significant period of time—without losing so many customers as to make the action unprofitable. Id. ¶18. This inference, in turn, has led the Court to find that the licensing of all Intel-compatible PC operating systems worldwide does in fact constitute the relevant market in the context of the plaintiffs' monopoly maintenance claim. Id.

The plaintiffs proved at trial that Microsoft possesses a dominant, persistent, and increasing share of the relevant market. Microsoft's share of the worldwide market for Intel-compatible PC operating systems currently exceeds ninety-five percent, and the firm's share would stand well above eighty percent even if the Mac OS were included in the market. Id. ¶35. The plaintiffs also proved that the applications barrier to entry protects Microsoft's dominant market share. Id. ¶¶36-52. This barrier ensures that no Intel-compatible PC operating system other than Windows can attract significant consumer demand, and the barrier would operate to the same effect even if Microsoft held its prices substantially above the competitive level for a protracted period of time. Id. Together, the proof of dominant market share and the existence of a substantial barrier to effective entry create the presumption that Microsoft enjoys monopoly power. . . .

At trial, Microsoft attempted to rebut the presumption of monopoly power with evidence of both putative constraints on its ability to exercise such power and behavior of its own that is supposedly inconsistent with the possession of monopoly power. None of the purported constraints, however, actually deprive Microsoft of "the ability (1) to price substantially above the competitive

31

¶312

level and (2) to persist in doing so for a significant period without erosion by new entry or expansion." IIA Phillip E. Areeda, Herbert Hovenkamp & John L. Solow, Antitrust Law ¶501, at 86 (1995) (emphasis in original); see Findings ¶¶57-60. Furthermore, neither Microsoft's efforts at technical innovation nor its pricing behavior is inconsistent with the possession of monopoly power. Id. ¶¶61-66.

Even if Microsoft's rebuttal had attenuated the presumption created by the prima facie showing of monopoly power, corroborative evidence of monopoly power abounds in this record: Neither Microsoft nor its OEM customers believe that the latter have—or will have anytime soon—even a single, commercially viable alternative to licensing Windows for pre-installation on their PCs. Id. ¶¶53-55; cf. [Rothery Storage & Van Co. v. Atlas Van Lines, Inc., 792 F.2d 210, 219 n.4 (D.C. Cir. 1986)] ("we assume that economic actors usually have accurate perceptions of economic realities"). Moreover, over the past several years, Microsoft has comported itself in a way that could only be consistent with rational behavior for a profit-maximizing firm if the firm knew that it possessed monopoly power, and if it was motivated by a desire to preserve the barrier to entry protecting that power. Findings ¶¶67, 99, 136, 141, 215-16, 241, 261-62, 286, 291, 330, 355, 393, 407.

In short, the proof of Microsoft's dominant, persistent market share protected by a substantial barrier to entry, together with Microsoft's failure to rebut that prima facie showing effectively and the additional indicia of monopoly power, have compelled the Court to find as fact that Microsoft enjoys monopoly power in the relevant market. Id. ¶33.

2. Maintenance of Monopoly Power by Anticompetitive Means

In a §2 case, once it is proved that the defendant possesses monopoly power in a relevant market, liability for monopolization depends on a showing that the defendant used anticompetitive methods to achieve or maintain its position. See *Grinnell*; *Kodak* (Scalia, J., dissenting); Intergraph Corp. v. Intel Corp., 195 F.3d 1346, 1353 (Fed. Cir. 1999). Prior cases have established an analytical approach to determining whether challenged conduct should be deemed anticompetitive in the context of a monopoly maintenance claim. The threshold question in this analysis is whether the defendant's conduct is "exclusionary"—that is, whether it has restricted significantly, or threatens to restrict significantly, the ability of other firms to compete in the relevant market on the merits of what they offer customers. See *Kodak* (Scalia, J., dissenting) (§2 is "directed to discrete situations" in which the behavior of

Microsoft Corp. ¶312

firms with monopoly power "threatens to defeat or forestall the corrective forces of competition").[1]

If the evidence reveals a significant exclusionary impact in the relevant market, the defendant's conduct will be labeled "anticompetitive"—and liability will attach—unless the defendant comes forward with specific, procompetitive business motivations that explain the full extent of its exclusionary conduct. See *Kodak* (declining to grant defendant's motion for summary judgment because factual questions remained as to whether defendant's asserted justifications were sufficient to explain the exclusionary conduct or were instead merely pretextual); see also *Aspen* (holding that the second element of a monopoly maintenance claim is satisfied by proof of "behavior that not only (1) tends to impair the opportunities of rivals, but also (2) either does not further competition on the merits or does so in an unnecessarily restrictive way") (quoting III Phillip E. Areeda & Donald F. Turner, Antitrust Law ¶626b, at 78 (1978)).

If the defendant with monopoly power consciously antagonized its customers by making its products less attractive to them—or if it incurred other costs, such as large outlays of development capital and forfeited opportunities to derive revenue from it—with no prospect of compensation other than the erection or preservation of barriers against competition by equally efficient firms, the Court may deem the defendant's conduct "predatory." As the D.C. Circuit stated in Neumann v. Reinforced Earth Co.,

> [P]redation involves aggression against business rivals through the use of business practices that would not be considered profit maximizing except for the expectation that (1) actual rivals will be driven from the market, or the entry of potential rivals blocked or delayed, so that the predator will gain or retain a market share sufficient to command monopoly profits, or (2) rivals will be chastened sufficiently to abandon competitive behavior the predator finds threatening to its realization of monopoly profits. [786 F.2d 424, 427 (D.C. Cir. 1986).]

Proof that a profit-maximizing firm took predatory action should suffice to demonstrate the threat of substantial exclusionary effect; to hold otherwise would be to ascribe irrational behavior to the defendant. Moreover, predatory conduct, by definition as well as by nature, lacks procompetitive business

---

[1] Proof that the defendant's conduct was motivated by a desire to prevent other firms from competing on the merits can contribute to a finding that the conduct has had, or will have, the intended, exclusionary effect. See *Gypsum* ("consideration of intent may play an important role in divining the actual nature and effect of the alleged anticompetitive conduct").

¶312 *Microsoft Corp.*

motivation. See *Aspen* (evidence indicating that defendant's conduct was "motivated entirely by a decision to avoid providing any benefits" to a rival supported the inference that defendant's conduct "was not motivated by efficiency concerns"). In other words, predatory behavior is patently anticompetitive. Proof that a firm with monopoly power engaged in such behavior thus necessitates a finding of liability under §2.

In this case, Microsoft early on recognized middleware as the Trojan horse that, once having, in effect, infiltrated the applications barrier, could enable rival operating systems to enter the market for Intel-compatible PC operating systems unimpeded. Simply put, middleware threatened to demolish Microsoft's coveted monopoly power. Alerted to the threat, Microsoft strove over a period of approximately four years to prevent middleware technologies from fostering the development of enough full-featured, cross-platform applications to erode the applications barrier. In pursuit of this goal, Microsoft sought to convince developers to concentrate on Windows-specific APIs and ignore interfaces exposed by the two incarnations of middleware that posed the greatest threat, namely, Netscape's Navigator Web browser and Sun's implementation of the Java technology. Microsoft's campaign succeeded in preventing—for several years, and perhaps permanently—Navigator and Java from fulfilling their potential to open the market for Intel-compatible PC operating systems to competition on the merits. Findings ¶¶133, 378. Because Microsoft achieved this result through exclusionary acts that lacked procompetitive justification, the Court deems Microsoft's conduct the maintenance of monopoly power by anticompetitive means.

a. Combating the Browser Threat

The same ambition that inspired Microsoft's efforts to induce Intel, Apple, RealNetworks and IBM to desist from certain technological innovations and business initiatives—namely, the desire to preserve the applications barrier—motivated the firm's June 1995 proposal that Netscape abstain from releasing platform-level browsing software for 32-bit versions of Windows. See id. ¶¶ 79-80, 93-132. This proposal, together with the punitive measures that Microsoft inflicted on Netscape when it rebuffed the overture, illuminates the context in which Microsoft's subsequent behavior toward PC manufacturers ("OEMs"), Internet access providers ("IAPs"), and other firms must be viewed.

When Netscape refused to abandon its efforts to develop Navigator into a

Microsoft Corp. ¶312

substantial platform for applications development, Microsoft focused its efforts on minimizing the extent to which developers would avail themselves of interfaces exposed by that nascent platform. Microsoft realized that the extent of developers' reliance on Netscape's browser platform would depend largely on the size and trajectory of Navigator's share of browser usage. Microsoft thus set out to maximize Internet Explorer's share of browser usage at Navigator's expense. Id. ¶¶133, 359-61. The core of this strategy was ensuring that the firms comprising the most effective channels for the generation of browser usage would devote their distributional and promotional efforts to Internet Explorer rather than Navigator. Recognizing that pre-installation by OEMs and bundling with the proprietary software of IAPs led more directly and efficiently to browser usage than any other practices in the industry, Microsoft devoted major efforts to usurping those two channels. Id. ¶143.

i. The OEM Channel

With respect to OEMs, Microsoft's campaign proceeded on three fronts. First, Microsoft bound Internet Explorer to Windows with contractual and, later, technological shackles in order to ensure the prominent (and ultimately permanent) presence of Internet Explorer on every Windows user's PC system, and to increase the costs attendant to installing and using Navigator on any PCs running Windows. Id. ¶¶155-74. Second, Microsoft imposed stringent limits on the freedom of OEMs to reconfigure or modify Windows 95 and Windows 98 in ways that might enable OEMs to generate usage for Navigator in spite of the contractual and technological devices that Microsoft had employed to bind Internet Explorer to Windows. Id. ¶¶202-29. Finally, Microsoft used incentives and threats to induce especially important OEMs to design their distributional, promotional and technical efforts to favor Internet Explorer to the exclusion of Navigator. Id. ¶¶230-38.

Microsoft's actions increased the likelihood that pre-installation of Navigator onto Windows would cause user confusion and system degradation, and therefore lead to higher support costs and reduced sales for the OEMs. Id. ¶¶159, 172. Not willing to take actions that would jeopardize their already slender profit margins, OEMs felt compelled by Microsoft's actions to reduce drastically their distribution and promotion of Navigator. Id. ¶¶239, 241. The substantial inducements that Microsoft held out to the largest OEMs only further reduced the distribution and promotion of Navigator in the OEM channel. Id. ¶¶230, 233. The response of OEMs to Microsoft's efforts had a dramatic, negative impact on Navigator's usage share. Id. ¶376. The drop

35

in usage share, in turn, has prevented Navigator from being the vehicle to open the relevant market to competition on the merits. Id. ¶¶377-78, 383.

Microsoft fails to advance any legitimate business objectives that actually explain the full extent of this significant exclusionary impact. The Court has already found that no quality-related or technical justifications fully explain Microsoft's refusal to license Windows 95 to OEMs without version 1.0 through 4.0 of Internet Explorer, or its refusal to permit them to uninstall versions 3.0 and 4.0. Id. ¶¶175-76. The same lack of justification applies to Microsoft's decision not to offer a browserless version of Windows 98 to consumers and OEMs, id. ¶177, as well as to its claim that it could offer "best of breed" implementations of functionalities in Web browsers. With respect to the latter assertion, Internet Explorer is not demonstrably the current "best of breed" Web browser, nor is it likely to be so at any time in the immediate future. The fact that Microsoft itself was aware of this reality only further strengthens the conclusion that Microsoft's decision to tie Internet Explorer to Windows cannot truly be explained as an attempt to benefit consumers and improve the efficiency of the software market generally, but rather as part of a larger campaign to quash innovation that threatened its monopoly position. Id. ¶¶195, 198.

To the extent that Microsoft still asserts a copyright defense, relying upon federal copyright law as a justification for its various restrictions on OEMs, that defense neither explains nor operates to immunize Microsoft's conduct under the Sherman Act. As a general proposition, Microsoft argues that the federal Copyright Act endows the holder of a valid copyright in software with an absolute right to prevent licensees, in this case the OEMs, from shipping modified versions of its product without its express permission. In truth, Windows 95 and Windows 98 are covered by copyright registrations, Findings ¶228, that "constitute prima facie evidence of the validity of the copyright." But the validity of Microsoft's copyrights has never been in doubt; the issue is what, precisely, they protect.

Microsoft has presented no evidence that the contractual (or the technological) restrictions it placed on OEMs' ability to alter Windows derive from any of the enumerated rights explicitly granted to a copyright holder under the Copyright Act. Instead, Microsoft argues that the restrictions "simply restate" an expansive right to preserve the "integrity" of its copyrighted software against any "distortion," "truncation," or "alteration," a right nowhere mentioned among the Copyright Act's list of exclusive rights, thus raising some doubt as to its existence. See Twentieth Century Music Corp. v. Aiken, 422

U.S. 151, 155 (1975) (not all uses of a work are within copyright holder's control; rights limited to specifically granted "exclusive rights"); cf. 17 U.S.C. §501(a) (infringement means violating specifically enumerated rights).[2]

It is also well settled that a copyright holder is not by reason thereof entitled to employ the perquisites in ways that directly threaten competition. See, e.g., *Kodak* ("The Court has held many times that power gained through some natural and legal advantage such as a . . . copyright, . . . can give rise to liability if 'a seller exploits his dominant position in one market to expand his empire into the next.' ") (quoting Times-Picayune Pub. Co. v. United States, 345 U.S. 594, 611, (1953)); Square D Co. v. Niagara Frontier Tariff Bureau, Inc., 476 U.S. 409, 421, (1986); Data General Corp. v. Grumman Systems Support Corp., 36 F.3d 1147, 1186 n.63 (1st Cir. 1994) (a copyright does not exempt its holder from antitrust inquiry where the copyright is used as part of a scheme to monopolize); see also Image Technical Services, Inc. v. Eastman Kodak Co., 125 F.3d 1195, 1219 (9th Cir. 1997), cert. denied, 523 U.S. 1094 ("Neither the aims of intellectual property law, nor the antitrust laws justify allowing a monopolist to rely upon a pretextual business justification to mask anticompetitive conduct."). Even constitutional privileges confer no immunity when they are abused for anticompetitive purposes. See *Lorain Journal*.

The Court has already found that the true impetus behind Microsoft's restrictions on OEMs was not its desire to maintain a somewhat amorphous quality it refers to as the "integrity" of the Windows platform, nor even to ensure that Windows afforded a uniform and stable platform for applications development. Microsoft itself engendered, or at least countenanced, instability and inconsistency by permitting Microsoft-friendly modifications to the desktop and boot sequence, and by releasing updates to Internet Explorer more frequently than it released new versions of Windows. Findings ¶226. Add to this the fact that the modifications OEMs desired to make would not have removed or altered any Windows APIs, and thus would not have disrupted any of Windows' functionalities, and it is apparent that Microsoft's conduct is effectively explained by its foreboding that OEMs would pre-install and give prominent placement to middleware like Navigator that could attract enough developer attention to weaken the applications barrier to

---

[2] While Microsoft is correct that some courts have also recognized the right of a copyright holder to preserve the "integrity" of artistic works in addition to those rights enumerated in the Copyright Act, the Court nevertheless concludes that those cases, being actions for infringement without antitrust implications, are inapposite to the one currently before it. See, e.g., WGN Continental Broadcasting Co. v. United Video, Inc., 693 F.2d 622 (7th Cir. 1982); Gilliam v. ABC, Inc., 538 F.2d 14 (2d Cir. 1976).

entry. Id. ¶227. In short, if Microsoft was truly inspired by a genuine concern for maximizing consumer satisfaction, as well as preserving its substantial investment in a worthy product, then it would have relied more on the power of the very competitive PC market, and less on its own market power, to prevent OEMs from making modifications that consumers did not want. Id. ¶¶225, 228-29.

ii. The IAP Channel

Microsoft adopted similarly aggressive measures to ensure that the IAP channel would generate browser usage share for Internet Explorer rather than Navigator. To begin with, Microsoft licensed Internet Explorer and the Internet Explorer Access Kit to hundreds of IAPs for no charge. Id. ¶¶250-51. Then, Microsoft extended valuable promotional treatment to the ten most important IAPs in exchange for their commitment to promote and distribute Internet Explorer and to exile Navigator from the desktop. Id. ¶¶255-58, 261, 272, 288-90, 305-06. Finally, in exchange for efforts to upgrade existing subscribers to client software that came bundled with Internet Explorer instead of Navigator, Microsoft granted rebates—and in some cases made outright payments—to those same IAPs. Id. ¶¶259-60, 295. Given the importance of the IAP channel to browser usage share, it is fair to conclude that these inducements and restrictions contributed significantly to the drastic changes that have in fact occurred in Internet Explorer's and Navigator's respective usage shares. Id. ¶¶144-47, 309-10. Microsoft's actions in the IAP channel thereby contributed significantly to preserving the applications barrier to entry.

There are no valid reasons to justify the full extent of Microsoft's exclusionary behavior in the IAP channel. A desire to limit free riding on the firm's investment in consumer-oriented features, such as the Referral Server and the Online Services Folder, can, in some circumstances, qualify as a procompetitive business motivation; but that motivation does not explain the full extent of the restrictions that Microsoft actually imposed upon IAPs. Under the terms of the agreements, an IAP's failure to keep Navigator shipments below the specified percentage primed Microsoft's contractual right to dismiss the IAP from its own favored position in the Referral Server or the Online Services Folder. This was true even if the IAP had refrained from promoting Navigator in its client software included with Windows, had purged all mention of Navigator from any Web site directly connected to the Referral Server, and had distributed no browser other than Internet Explorer

Microsoft Corp. ¶312

to the new subscribers it gleaned from the Windows desktop. Id. ¶¶258, 262, 289. Thus, Microsoft's restrictions closed off a substantial amount of distribution that would not have constituted a free ride to Navigator.

Nor can an ostensibly procompetitive desire to "foster brand association" explain the full extent of Microsoft's restrictions. If Microsoft's only concern had been brand association, restrictions on the ability of IAPs to promote Navigator likely would have sufficed. It is doubtful that Microsoft would have paid IAPs to induce their existing subscribers to drop Navigator in favor of Internet Explorer unless it was motivated by a desire to extinguish Navigator as a threat. See id. ¶¶259, 295. More generally, it is crucial to an understanding of Microsoft's intentions to recognize that Microsoft paid for the fealty of IAPs with large investments in software development for their benefit, conceded opportunities to take a profit, suffered competitive disadvantage to Microsoft's own OLS, and gave outright bounties. Id. ¶¶259-60, 277, 284-86, 295. Considering that Microsoft never intended to derive appreciable revenue from Internet Explorer directly, id. ¶¶136-37, these sacrifices could only have represented rational business judgments to the extent that they promised to diminish Navigator's share of browser usage and thereby contribute significantly to eliminating a threat to the applications barrier to entry. Id. ¶291. Because the full extent of Microsoft's exclusionary initiatives in the IAP channel can only be explained by the desire to hinder competition on the merits in the relevant market, those initiatives must be labeled anticompetitive.

In sum, the efforts Microsoft directed at OEMs and IAPs successfully ostracized Navigator as a practical matter from the two channels that lead most efficiently to browser usage. Even when viewed independently, these two prongs of Microsoft's campaign threatened to "forestall the corrective forces of competition" and thereby perpetuate Microsoft's monopoly power in the relevant market. *Kodak* (Scalia, J., dissenting). Therefore, whether they are viewed separately or together, the OEM and IAP components of Microsoft's anticompetitive campaign merit a finding of liability under §2.

iii. ICPs, ISVs and Apple

No other distribution channels for browsing software approach the efficiency of OEM pre-installation and IAP bundling. Findings ¶¶144-47. Nevertheless, protecting the applications barrier to entry was so critical to Microsoft that the firm was willing to invest substantial resources to enlist ICPs, ISVs, and Apple in its campaign against the browser threat. By extracting from Apple terms that significantly diminished the usage of Navigator on the Mac OS, Microsoft helped to ensure that developers would not view Navigator as truly cross-platform middleware. Id. ¶356. By granting ICPs and ISVs free licenses to bundle Internet Explorer with their offerings, and by exchanging other valuable inducements for their agreement to distribute, promote and rely on Internet Explorer rather than Navigator, Microsoft directly induced developers to focus on its own APIs rather than ones exposed by Navigator. Id. ¶¶334-35, 340. These measures supplemented Microsoft's efforts in the OEM and IAP channels.

Just as they fail to account for the measures that Microsoft took in the IAP channel, the goals of preventing free riding and preserving brand association fail to explain the full extent of Microsoft's actions in the ICP channel. Id. ¶¶329-30. With respect to the ISV agreements, Microsoft has put forward no procompetitive business ends whatsoever to justify their exclusionary terms. See id. ¶¶339-40. Finally, Microsoft's willingness to make the sacrifices involved in canceling Mac Office, and the concessions relating to browsing software that it demanded from Apple, can only be explained by Microsoft's desire to protect the applications barrier to entry from the threat posed by Navigator. Id. ¶355. Thus, once again, Microsoft is unable to justify the full extent of its restrictive behavior.

b. Combating the Java Threat

As part of its grand strategy to protect the applications barrier, Microsoft employed an array of tactics designed to maximize the difficulty with which applications written in Java could be ported from Windows to other platforms, and vice versa. The first of these measures was the creation of a Java implementation for Windows that undermined portability and was incompatible with other implementations. Id. ¶¶387-93. Microsoft then induced developers to use its implementation of Java rather than Sun-compliant ones. It pursued this tactic directly, by means of subterfuge and barter, and indirectly, through its campaign to minimize Navigator's usage share. Id. ¶¶394, 396-97, 399-400, 401-03. In a separate effort to prevent the development of easily portable Java applications, Microsoft used its monopoly power to prevent firms such as Intel from aiding in the creation of cross-platform interfaces. Id. ¶¶404-06.

Microsoft's tactics induced many Java developers to write their applications using Microsoft's developer tools and to refrain from distributing Sun-compliant JVMs [Java virtual machines] to Windows users. This stratagem has effectively resulted in fewer applications that are easily portable. Id.

Microsoft Corp. ¶312

¶398. What is more, Microsoft's actions interfered with the development of new cross-platform Java interfaces. Id. ¶406. It is not clear whether, absent Microsoft's machinations, Sun's Java efforts would by now have facilitated porting between Windows and other platforms to a degree sufficient to render the applications barrier to entry vulnerable. It is clear, however, that Microsoft's actions markedly impeded Java's progress to that end. Id. ¶407. The evidence thus compels the conclusion that Microsoft's actions with respect to Java have restricted significantly the ability of other firms to compete on the merits in the market for Intel-compatible PC operating systems.

Microsoft's actions to counter the Java threat went far beyond the development of an attractive alternative to Sun's implementation of the technology. Specifically, Microsoft successfully pressured Intel, which was dependent in many ways on Microsoft's good graces, to abstain from aiding in Sun's and Netscape's Java development work. Id. ¶¶396, 406. Microsoft also deliberately designed its Java development tools so that developers who were opting for portability over performance would nevertheless unwittingly write Java applications that would run only on Windows. Id. ¶394. Moreover, Microsoft's means of luring developers to its Java implementation included maximizing Internet Explorer's share of browser usage at Navigator's expense in ways the Court has already held to be anticompetitive. See supra, §I.A.2.a. Finally, Microsoft impelled ISVs, which are dependent upon Microsoft for technical information and certifications relating to Windows, to use and distribute Microsoft's version of the Windows JVM rather than any Sun-compliant version. Id. ¶¶401-03.

These actions cannot be described as competition on the merits, and they did not benefit consumers. In fact, Microsoft's actions did not even benefit Microsoft in the short run, for the firm's efforts to create incompatibility between its JVM for Windows and others' JVMs for Windows resulted in fewer total applications being able to run on Windows than otherwise would have been written. Microsoft was willing nevertheless to obstruct the development of Windows-compatible applications if they would be easy to port to other platforms and would thus diminish the applications barrier to entry. Id. ¶407.

c. Microsoft's Conduct Taken As a Whole

As the foregoing discussion illustrates, Microsoft's campaign to protect the applications barrier from erosion by network-centric middleware can be broken down into discrete categories of activity, several of which on their own independently satisfy the second element of a §2 monopoly maintenance claim. But only when the separate categories of conduct are viewed, as they should be, as a single, well-coordinated course of action does the full extent of the violence that Microsoft has done to the competitive process reveal itself. See Continental Ore Co. v. Union Carbide & Carbon Corp., 370 U.S. 690, 699 (1962) (counseling that in Sherman Act cases "plaintiffs should be given the full benefit of their proof without tightly compartmentalizing the various factual components and wiping the slate clean after scrutiny of each"). In essence, Microsoft mounted a deliberate assault upon entrepreneurial efforts that, left to rise or fall on their own merits, could well have enabled the introduction of competition into the market for Intel-compatible PC operating systems. Id. ¶411. While the evidence does not prove that they would have succeeded absent Microsoft's actions, it does reveal that Microsoft placed an oppressive thumb on the scale of competitive fortune, thereby effectively guaranteeing its continued dominance in the relevant market. More broadly, Microsoft's anticompetitive actions trammeled the competitive process through which the computer software industry generally stimulates innovation and conduces to the optimum benefit of consumers. Id. ¶412.

Viewing Microsoft's conduct as a whole also reinforces the conviction that it was predacious. Microsoft paid vast sums of money, and renounced many millions more in lost revenue every year, in order to induce firms to take actions that would help enhance Internet Explorer's share of browser usage at Navigator's expense. Id. ¶139. These outlays cannot be explained as subventions to maximize return from Internet Explorer. Microsoft has no intention of ever charging for licenses to use or distribute its browser. Id. ¶¶137-38. Moreover, neither the desire to bolster demand for Windows nor the prospect of ancillary revenues from Internet Explorer can explain the lengths to which Microsoft has gone. In fact, Microsoft has expended wealth and foresworn opportunities to realize more in a manner and to an extent that can only represent a rational investment if its purpose was to perpetuate the applications barrier to entry. Id. ¶¶136, 139-42. Because Microsoft's business practices "would not be considered profit maximizing except for the expectation that . . . the entry of potential rivals" into the market for Intel-compatible PC operating systems will be "blocked or delayed," Neumann v. Reinforced Earth Co., 786 F.2d 424, 427 (D.C. Cir. 1986), Microsoft's campaign must be termed predatory. Since the Court has already found that Microsoft possesses monopoly power, see supra, §I.A.1, the predatory nature of the firm's conduct compels the Court to hold Microsoft liable under §2 of the Sherman Act.

Microsoft Corp. ¶312

B. Attempting to Obtain Monopoly Power in a Second Market by Anticompetitive Means

In addition to condemning actual monopolization, §2 of the Sherman Act declares that it is unlawful for a person or firm to "attempt to monopolize . . . any part of the trade or commerce among the several States, or with foreign nations. . . ." Relying on this language, the plaintiffs assert that Microsoft's anticompetitive efforts to maintain its monopoly power in the market for Intel-compatible PC operating systems warrant additional liability as an illegal attempt to amass monopoly power in "the browser market." The Court agrees.

In order for liability to attach for attempted monopolization, a plaintiff generally must prove "(1) that the defendant has engaged in predatory or anticompetitive conduct with (2) a specific intent to monopolize," and (3) that there is a "dangerous probability" that the defendant will succeed in achieving monopoly power. *Spectrum Sports.* Microsoft's June 1995 proposal that Netscape abandon the field to Microsoft in the market for browsing technology for Windows, and its subsequent, well-documented efforts to overwhelm Navigator's browser usage share with a proliferation of Internet Explorer browsers inextricably attached to Windows, clearly meet the first element of the offense.

The evidence in this record also satisfies the requirement of specific intent. Microsoft's effort to convince Netscape to stop developing platform-level browsing software for the 32-bit versions of Windows was made with full knowledge that Netscape's acquiescence in this market allocation scheme would, without more, have left Internet Explorer with such a large share of browser usage as to endow Microsoft with de facto monopoly power in the browser market. Findings ¶¶79-89.

When Netscape refused to abandon the development of browsing software for 32-bit versions of Windows, Microsoft's strategy for protecting the applications barrier became one of expanding Internet Explorer's share of browser usage—and simultaneously depressing Navigator's share—to an extent sufficient to demonstrate to developers that Navigator would never emerge as the standard software employed to browse the Web. Id. ¶133. While Microsoft's top executives never expressly declared acquisition of monopoly power in the browser market to be the objective, they knew, or should have known, that the tactics they actually employed were likely to push Internet Explorer's share to those extreme heights. Navigator's slow demise would leave a competitive vacuum for only Internet Explorer to fill. Yet, there is no evidence that Microsoft tried—or even considered trying—to prevent its anticompeti-

43

tive campaign from achieving overkill. Under these circumstances, it is fair to presume that the wrongdoer intended "the probable consequences of its acts." IIIA Phillip E. Areeda & Herbert Hovenkamp, Antitrust Law ¶805b, at 324 (1996); see also *Spectrum Sports* (proof of " 'predatory' tactics . . . may be sufficient to prove the necessary intent to monopolize, which is something more than an intent to compete vigorously"). Therefore, the facts of this case suffice to prove the element of specific intent.

Even if the first two elements of the offense are met, however, a defendant may not be held liable for attempted monopolization absent proof that its anticompetitive conduct created a dangerous probability of achieving the objective of monopoly power in a relevant market. Id. The evidence supports the conclusion that Microsoft's actions did pose such a danger.

At the time Microsoft presented its market allocation proposal to Netscape, Navigator's share of browser usage stood well above seventy percent, and no other browser enjoyed more than a fraction of the remainder. Findings ¶¶89, 372. Had Netscape accepted Microsoft's offer, nearly all of its share would have devolved upon Microsoft, because at that point, no potential third-party competitor could either claim to rival Netscape's stature as a browser company or match Microsoft's ability to leverage monopoly power in the market for Intel-compatible PC operating systems. In the time it would have taken an aspiring entrant to launch a serious effort to compete against Internet Explorer, Microsoft could have erected the same type of barrier that protects its existing monopoly power by adding proprietary extensions to the browsing software under its control and by extracting commitments from OEMs, IAPs and others similar to the ones discussed in §I.A.2, supra. In short, Netscape's assent to Microsoft's market division proposal would have, instanter, resulted in Microsoft's attainment of monopoly power in a second market. It follows that the proposal itself created a dangerous probability of that result. See United States v. American Airlines, Inc., 743 F.2d 1114, 1118-19 (5th Cir. 1984) (the fact that two executives "arguably" could have implemented market-allocation scheme that would have engendered monopoly power was sufficient for finding of dangerous probability). Although the dangerous probability was no longer imminent with Netscape's rejection of Microsoft's proposal, "the probability of success at the time the acts occur" is the measure by which liability is determined. Id. at 1118.

This conclusion alone is sufficient to support a finding of liability for attempted monopolization. The Court is nonetheless compelled to express its further conclusion that the predatory course of conduct Microsoft has pursued since June of 1995 has revived the dangerous probability that Microsoft will

Microsoft Corp. ¶312

attain monopoly power in a second market. Internet Explorer's share of browser usage has already risen above fifty percent, will exceed sixty percent by January 2001, and the trend continues unabated. Findings ¶¶372-73; see *M & M Medical Supplies & Serv., Inc. v. Pleasant Valley Hosp., Inc.*, 981 F.2d 160, 168 (4th Cir. 1992) (en banc) ("A rising share may show more probability of success than a falling share. . . . [C]laims involving greater than 50% share should be treated as attempts at monopolization when the other elements for attempted monopolization are also satisfied.") (citations omitted); see also IIIA Phillip E. Areeda & Herbert Hovenkamp, Antitrust Law ¶807d, at 354-55 (1996) (acknowledging the significance of a large, rising market share to the dangerous probability element).

II. SECTION ONE OF THE SHERMAN ACT . . .

A. Tying

Liability for tying under §1 exists where (1) two separate "products" are involved; (2) the defendant affords its customers no choice but to take the tied product in order to obtain the tying product; (3) the arrangement affects a substantial volume of interstate commerce; and (4) the defendant has "market power" in the tying product market. *Jefferson Parish*. The Supreme Court has since reaffirmed this test in *Kodak*. All four elements are required, whether the arrangement is subjected to a per se or Rule of Reason analysis.

The plaintiffs allege that Microsoft's combination of Windows and Internet Explorer by contractual and technological artifices constitute unlawful tying to the extent that those actions forced Microsoft's customers and consumers to take Internet Explorer as a condition of obtaining Windows. While the Court agrees with plaintiffs, and thus holds that Microsoft is liable for illegal tying under §1, this conclusion is arguably at variance with a decision of the U.S. Court of Appeals for the D.C. Circuit in a closely related case, and must therefore be explained in some detail. Whether the decisions are indeed inconsistent is not for this Court to say.

The decision of the D.C. Circuit in question is *United States v. Microsoft Corp.*, 147 F.3d 935 (D.C. Cir. 1998) ("*Microsoft II*") which is itself related to an earlier decision of the same Circuit, *United States v. Microsoft Corp.*, 56 F.3d 1448 (D.C. Cir. 1995) ("*Microsoft I*"). The history of the controversy is sufficiently set forth in the appellate opinions and need not be recapitulated here, except to state that those decisions anticipated the instant case, and that *Microsoft II* sought to guide this Court, insofar as practicable, in the further proceedings it fully expected to ensue on the tying issue. Nevertheless, upon

¶312

reflection this Court does not believe the D.C. Circuit intended *Microsoft II* to state a controlling rule of law for purposes of this case. As the *Microsoft II* court itself acknowledged, the issue before it was the construction to be placed upon a single provision of a consent decree that, although animated by antitrust considerations, was nevertheless still primarily a matter of determining contractual intent. The court of appeals' observations on the extent to which software product design decisions may be subject to judicial scrutiny in the course of §1 tying cases are in the strictest sense obiter dicta, and are thus not formally binding. Nevertheless, both prudence and the deference this Court owes to pronouncements of its own Circuit oblige that it follow in the direction it is pointed until the trail falters.

The majority opinion in *Microsoft II* evinces both an extraordinary degree of respect for changes (including "integration") instigated by designers of technological products, such as software, in the name of product "improvement," and a corresponding lack of confidence in the ability of the courts to distinguish between improvements in fact and improvements in name only, made for anticompetitive purposes. Read literally, the D.C. Circuit's opinion appears to immunize any product design (or, at least, software product design) from antitrust scrutiny, irrespective of its effect upon competition, if the software developer can postulate any "plausible claim" of advantage to its arrangement of code.

This undemanding test appears to this Court to be inconsistent with the pertinent Supreme Court precedents in at least three respects. First, it views the market from the defendant's perspective, or, more precisely, as the defendant would like to have the market viewed. Second, it ignores reality: The claim of advantage need only be plausible; it need not be proved. Third, it dispenses with any balancing of the hypothetical advantages against any anticompetitive effects.

The two most recent Supreme Court cases to have addressed the issue of product and market definition in the context of Sherman Act tying claims are *Jefferson Parish* and *Kodak*. In *Jefferson Parish*, the Supreme Court held that a hospital offering hospital services and anesthesiology services as a package could not be found to have violated the anti-tying rules unless the evidence established that patients, i.e. consumers, perceived the services as separate products for which they desired a choice, and that the package had the effect of forcing the patients to purchase an unwanted product. In *Kodak* the Supreme Court held that a manufacturer of photocopying and micrographic equipment, in agreeing to sell replacement parts for its machines only to those customers who also agreed to purchase repair services from it as well, would be guilty of tying if the evidence at trial established the existence of consumer demand for parts and services separately.

Both defendants asserted, as Microsoft does here, that the tied and tying products were in reality only a single product, or that every item was traded in a single market.[3] In *Jefferson Parish*, the defendant contended that it offered a "functionally integrated package of services"—a single product— but the Supreme Court concluded that the "character of the demand" for the constituent components, not their functional relationship, determined whether separate "products" were actually involved. In *Kodak*, the defendant postulated that effective competition in the equipment market precluded the possibility of the use of market power anticompetitively in any after-markets for parts or services: Sales of machines, parts, and services were all responsive to the discipline of the larger equipment market. The Supreme Court declined to accept this premise in the absence of evidence of "actual market realities," ultimately holding that "the proper market definition in this case can be determined only after a factual inquiry into the 'commercial realities' faced by consumers."[4]

In both *Jefferson Parish* and *Kodak*, the Supreme Court also gave consideration to certain theoretical "valid business reasons" proffered by the defendants as to why the arrangements should be deemed benign. In *Jefferson Parish*, the hospital asserted that the combination of hospital and anesthesia services eliminated multiple problems of scheduling, supply, performance standards, and equipment maintenance. The manufacturer in *Kodak* contended that quality control, inventory management, and the prevention of free riding justified its decision to sell parts only in conjunction with service. In neither case did the Supreme Court find those justifications sufficient if anticompetitive effects were proved.... Thus, at a minimum, the admonition of the D.C. Circuit in *Microsoft II* to refrain from any product design assessment as to whether the "integration" of Windows and Internet Explorer is a "net plus," deferring to Microsoft's "plausible claim" that it is of "some advantage" to consumers, is at odds with the Supreme Court's own approach.

The significance of those cases, for this Court's purposes, is to teach that

---

[3]Microsoft contends that Windows and Internet Explorer represent a single "integrated product," and that the relevant market is a unitary market of "platforms for software applications."

[4]In *Microsoft II* the D.C. Circuit acknowledged it was without benefit of a complete factual record which might alter its conclusion that the "Windows 95/IE package is a genuine integration."

¶312

resolution of product and market definitional problems must depend upon proof of commercial reality, as opposed to what might appear to be reasonable. In both cases the Supreme Court instructed that product and market definitions were to be ascertained by reference to evidence of consumers' perception of the nature of the products and the markets for them, rather than to abstract or metaphysical assumptions as to the configuration of the "product" and the "market." *Jefferson Parish*; *Kodak*. In the instant case, the commercial reality is that consumers today perceive operating systems and browsers as separate "products," for which there is separate demand. Findings ¶¶149-54. This is true notwithstanding the fact that the software code supplying their discrete functionalities can be commingled in virtually infinite combinations, rendering each indistinguishable from the whole in terms of files of code or any other taxonomy. Id. ¶¶149-50, 162-63, 187-91.

Proceeding in line with the Supreme Court cases, which are indisputably controlling, this Court first concludes that Microsoft possessed "appreciable economic power in the tying market," *Kodak*, which in this case is the market for Intel-compatible PC operating systems. See *Jefferson Parish* (defining market power as ability to force purchaser to do something that he would not do in competitive market); see also Fortner Enterprises, Inc. v. United States Steel Corp., 394 U.S. 495, 504 (1969) (ability to raise prices or to impose tie-ins on any appreciable number of buyers within the tying product market is sufficient). While courts typically have not specified a percentage of the market that creates the presumption of "market power," no court has ever found that the requisite degree of power exceeds the amount necessary for a finding of monopoly power. See *Kodak*. Because this Court has already found that Microsoft possesses monopoly power in the worldwide market for Intel-compatible PC operating systems (i.e., the tying product market), Findings ¶¶18-67, the threshold element of "appreciable economic power" is a fortiori met.

Similarly, the Court's Findings strongly support a conclusion that a "not insubstantial" amount of commerce was foreclosed to competitors as a result of Microsoft's decision to bundle Internet Explorer with Windows. The controlling consideration under this element is "simply whether a total amount of business" that is "substantial enough in terms of dollar-volume so as not to be merely de minimis" is foreclosed. Fortner, 394 U.S. at 501, 89 S. Ct. 1252; cf. *International Salt* (unreasonable per se to foreclose competitors from any substantial market by a tying arrangement).

Although the Court's Findings do not specify a dollar amount of business that has been foreclosed to any particular present or potential competitor of

Microsoft in the relevant market,[5] including Netscape, the Court did find that Microsoft's bundling practices caused Navigator's usage share to drop substantially from 1995 to 1998, and that as a direct result Netscape suffered a severe drop in revenues from lost advertisers, Web traffic and purchases of server products. It is thus obvious that the foreclosure achieved by Microsoft's refusal to offer Internet Explorer separately from Windows exceeds the Supreme Court's de minimis threshold. See *Digidyne Corp. v. Data General Corp.*, 734 F.2d 1336, 1341 (9th Cir. 1984) (citing *Fortner*).

The facts of this case also prove the elements of the forced bundling requirement. Indeed, the Supreme Court has stated that the "essential characteristic" of an illegal tying arrangement is a seller's decision to exploit its market power over the tying product "to force the buyer into the purchase of a tied product that the buyer either did not want at all, or might have preferred to purchase elsewhere on different terms." *Jefferson Parish*. In that regard, the Court has found that, beginning with the early agreements for Windows 95, Microsoft has conditioned the provision of a license to distribute Windows on the OEMs' purchase of Internet Explorer. Findings ¶¶158-65. The agreements prohibited the licensees from ever modifying or deleting any part of Windows, despite the OEMs' expressed desire to be allowed to do so. Id. ¶¶158, 164. As a result, OEMs were generally not permitted, with only one brief exception, to satisfy consumer demand for a browserless version of Windows 95 without Internet Explorer. Id. ¶¶158, 202. Similarly, Microsoft refused to license Windows 98 to OEMs unless they also agreed to abstain from removing the icons for Internet Explorer from the desktop. Id. ¶213. Consumers were also effectively compelled to purchase Internet Explorer along with Windows 98 by Microsoft's decision to stop including Internet Explorer on the list of programs subject to the Add/Remove function and by its decision not to respect their selection of another browser as their default. Id. ¶¶170-72.

The fact that Microsoft ostensibly priced Internet Explorer at zero does not detract from the conclusion that consumers were forced to pay, one way or another, for the browser along with Windows. Despite Microsoft's assertion that the Internet Explorer technologies are not "purchased" since they are included in a single royalty price paid by OEMs for Windows 98, it is nevertheless clear that licensees, including consumers, are forced to take, and pay for, the entire package of software and that any value to be ascribed to Inter-

---

[5]Most of the quantitative evidence was presented in units other than monetary, but numbered the units in millions, whatever their nature.

¶312

net Explorer is built into this single price. See United States v. Microsoft Corp., Nos. CIV. A. 98-1232, 98-1233, 1998 WL 614485, *12 (D.D.C., Sept. 14, 1998); IIIA Philip E. Areeda & Herbert Hovenkamp, Antitrust Law ¶760b6, at 51 (1996) ("[T]he tie may be obvious, as in the classic form, or somewhat more subtle, as when a machine is sold or leased at a price that covers 'free' servicing."). Moreover, the purpose of the Supreme Court's "forcing" inquiry is to expose those product bundles that raise the cost or difficulty of doing business for would-be competitors to prohibitively high levels, thereby depriving consumers of the opportunity to evaluate a competing product on its relative merits. It is not, as Microsoft suggests, simply to punish firms on the basis of an increment in price attributable to the tied product. See Fortner, 394 U.S. at 512-14 (1969); *Jefferson Parish*.

As for the crucial requirement that Windows and Internet Explorer be deemed "separate products" for a finding of technological tying liability, this Court's Findings mandate such a conclusion. Considering the "character of demand" for the two products, as opposed to their "functional relation," id. at 19, Web browsers and operating systems are "distinguishable in the eyes of buyers." Id.; Findings ¶¶149-54. Consumers often base their choice of which browser should reside on their operating system on their individual demand for the specific functionalities or characteristics of a particular browser, separate and apart from the functionalities afforded by the operating system itself. Id. ¶¶149-51. Moreover, the behavior of other, lesser software vendors confirms that it is certainly efficient to provide an operating system and a browser separately, or at least in separable form. Id. ¶153. Microsoft is the only firm to refuse to license its operating system without a browser. Id.; see *Berkey Photo*. This Court concludes that Microsoft's decision to offer only the bundled—"integrated"—version of Windows and Internet Explorer derived not from technical necessity or business efficiencies; rather, it was the result of a deliberate and purposeful choice to quell incipient competition before it reached truly minatory proportions.

The Court is fully mindful of the reasons for the admonition of the D.C. Circuit in *Microsoft II* of the perils associated with a rigid application of the traditional "separate products" test to computer software design. Given the virtually infinite malleability of software code, software upgrades and new application features, such as Web browsers, could virtually always be configured so as to be capable of separate and subsequent installation by an immediate licensee or end user. A court mechanically applying a strict "separate demand" test could improvidently wind up condemning "integrations" that represent genuine improvements to software that are benign from the standpoint of consumer welfare and a competitive market. Clearly, this is not a desirable outcome. Similar concerns have motivated other courts, as well as the D.C. Circuit, to resist a strict application of the "separate products" tests to similar questions of "technological tying." . . .

To the extent that the Supreme Court has spoken authoritatively on these issues, however, this Court is bound to follow its guidance and is not at liberty to extrapolate a new rule governing the tying of software products. Nevertheless, the Court is confident that its conclusion, limited by the unique circumstances of this case, is consistent with the Supreme Court's teaching to date.[6]

B. Exclusive Dealing Arrangements

Microsoft's various contractual agreements with some OLSs, ICPs, ISVs, Compaq and Apple are also called into question by plaintiffs as exclusive dealing arrangements under the language in §1 prohibiting "contract[s] . . . in restraint of trade or commerce. . . ." As detailed in §I.A.2, supra, each of these agreements with Microsoft required the other party to promote and distribute Internet Explorer to the partial or complete exclusion of Navigator. In exchange, Microsoft offered, to some or all of these parties, promotional patronage, substantial financial subsidies, technical support, and other valuable consideration. Under the clear standards established by the Supreme Court, these types of "vertical restrictions" are subject to a Rule of Reason analysis. See *Sylvania*; *Jefferson Parish*; cf. *Business Electronics* (holding that Rule of Reason analysis presumptively applies to cases brought under §1 of the Sherman Act).

Acknowledging that some exclusive dealing arrangements may have benign objectives and may create significant economic benefits, see *Tampa Electric*, courts have tended to condemn under the §1 Rule of Reason test only those agreements that have the effect of foreclosing a competing manu-

---

[6] . . . [T]he true source of the threat posed to the competitive process by Microsoft's bundling decisions stems from the fact that a competitor to the tied product bore the potential, but had not yet matured sufficiently, to open up the tying product market to competition. Under these conditions, the anticompetitive harm from a software bundle is much more substantial and pernicious than the typical tie. See X Phillip E. Areeda, Einer Elhauge & Herbert Hovenkamp, Antitrust Law ¶1747 (1996). A company able to leverage its substantial power in the tying product market in order to force consumers to accept a tie of partial substitutes is thus able to spread inefficiency from one market to the next, id. at 232, and thereby "sabotage a nascent technology that might compete with the tying product but for its foreclosure from the market." III Phillip E. Areeda & Herbert Hovenkamp, Antitrust Law ¶1746.1d at 495 (Supp.1999).

¶312 *Microsoft Corp.*

facturer's brands from the relevant market. More specifically, courts are concerned with those exclusive dealing arrangements that work to place so much of a market's available distribution outlets in the hands of a single firm as to make it difficult for other firms to continue to compete effectively, or even to exist, in the relevant market. See U.S. Healthcare Inc. v. Healthsource, Inc., 986 F.2d 589, 595 (1st Cir. 1993); Interface Group, Inc. v. Massachusetts Port Authority, 816 F.2d 9, 11 (1st Cir. 1987) (relying upon III Phillip E. Areeda & Donald F. Turner, Antitrust Law ¶732 (1978), *Tampa Electric,* and *Standard Stations*).

To evaluate an agreement's likely anticompetitive effects, courts have consistently looked at a variety of factors, including: (1) the degree of exclusivity and the relevant line of commerce implicated by the agreements' terms; (2) whether the percentage of the market foreclosed by the contracts is substantial enough to import that rivals will be largely excluded from competition; (3) the agreements' actual anticompetitive effect in the relevant line of commerce; (4) the existence of any legitimate, procompetitive business justifications offered by the defendant; (5) the length and irrevocability of the agreements; and (6) the availability of any less restrictive means for achieving the same benefits. See, e.g., *Tampa Electric*; Roland Machinery Co. v. Dresser Industries, Inc., 749 F.2d 380, 392-95 (7th Cir. 1984); see also XI Herbert Hovenkamp, Antitrust Law ¶1820 (1998).

Where courts have found that the agreements in question failed to foreclose absolutely outlets that together accounted for a substantial percentage of the total distribution of the relevant products, they have consistently declined to assign liability. See, e.g., id. ¶1821; U.S. Healthcare, 986 F.2d at 596-97; Roland Mach. Co., 749 F.2d at 394 (failure of plaintiff to meet threshold burden of proving that exclusive dealing arrangement is likely to keep at least one significant competitor from doing business in relevant market dictates no liability under §1). This Court has previously observed that the case law suggests that, unless the evidence demonstrates that Microsoft's agreements excluded Netscape altogether from access to roughly forty percent of the browser market, the Court should decline to find such agreements in violation of §1. See United States v. Microsoft Corp., Nos. CIV. A. 98-1232, 98-1233, 1998 WL 614485, at *19 (D.D.C. Sept. 14, 1998) (citing cases that tended to converge upon forty percent foreclosure rate for finding of §1 liability).

The only agreements revealed by the evidence which could be termed so "exclusive" as to merit scrutiny under the §1 Rule of Reason test are the agreements Microsoft signed with Compaq, AOL and several other OLSs, the

Microsoft Corp. ¶312

top ICPs, the leading ISVs, and Apple. The Findings of Fact also establish that, among the OEMs discussed supra, Compaq was the only one to fully commit itself to Microsoft's terms for distributing and promoting Internet Explorer to the exclusion of Navigator. Beginning with its decisions in 1996 and 1997 to promote Internet Explorer exclusively for its PC products, Compaq essentially ceased to distribute or pre-install Navigator at all in exchange for significant financial remuneration from Microsoft. Findings ¶¶230-34. AOL's March 12 and October 28, 1996 agreements with Microsoft also guaranteed that, for all practical purposes, Internet Explorer would be AOL's browser of choice, to be distributed and promoted through AOL's dominant, flagship online service, thus leaving Navigator to fend for itself. Id. ¶¶287-90, 293-97. In light of the severe shipment quotas and promotional restrictions for third-party browsers imposed by the agreements, the fact that Microsoft still permitted AOL to offer Navigator through a few subsidiary channels does not negate this conclusion. The same conclusion as to exclusionary effect can be drawn with respect to Microsoft's agreements with AT&T WorldNet, Prodigy and CompuServe, since those contract terms were almost identical to the ones contained in AOL's March 1996 agreement. Id. ¶¶305-06.

Microsoft also successfully induced some of the most popular ICPs and ISVs to commit to promote, distribute and utilize Internet Explorer technologies exclusively in their Web content in exchange for valuable placement on the Windows desktop and technical support. Specifically, the "Top Tier" and "Platinum" agreements that Microsoft formed with thirty-four of the most popular ICPs on the Web ensured that Navigator was effectively shut out of these distribution outlets for a significant period of time. Id. ¶¶317-22, 325-26, 332. In the same way, Microsoft's "First Wave" contracts provided crucial technical information to dozens of leading ISVs that agreed to make their Web-centric applications completely reliant on technology specific to Internet Explorer. Id. ¶¶337, 339-40. Finally, Apple's 1997 Technology Agreement with Microsoft prohibited Apple from actively promoting any non-Microsoft browsing software in any way or from pre-installing a browser other than Internet Explorer. Id. ¶¶350-52. This arrangement eliminated all meaningful avenues of distribution of Navigator through Apple. Id.

Notwithstanding the extent to which these "exclusive" distribution agreements preempted the most efficient channels for Navigator to achieve browser usage share, however, the Court concludes that Microsoft's multiple agreements with distributors did not ultimately deprive Netscape of the ability to have access to every PC user worldwide to offer an opportunity to install Navigator. Navigator can be downloaded from the Internet. It is available

¶312 *Microsoft Corp.*

through myriad retail channels. It can [be] (and has been) mailed directly to an unlimited number of households. How precisely it managed to do so is not shown by the evidence, but in 1998 alone, for example, Netscape was able to distribute 160 million copies of Navigator, contributing to an increase in its installed base from 15 million in 1996 to 33 million in December 1998. Id. ¶378. As such, the evidence does not support a finding that these agreements completely excluded Netscape from any constituent portion of the worldwide browser market, the relevant line of commerce.

The fact that Microsoft's arrangements with various firms did not foreclose enough of the relevant market to constitute a §1 violation in no way detracts from the Court's assignment of liability for the same arrangements under §2. As noted above, all of Microsoft's agreements, including the non-exclusive ones, severely restricted Netscape's access to those distribution channels leading most efficiently to the acquisition of browser usage share. They thus rendered Netscape harmless as a platform threat and preserved Microsoft's operating system monopoly, in violation of §2. But virtually all the leading case authority dictates that liability under §1 must hinge upon whether Netscape was actually shut out of the Web browser market, or at least whether it was forced to reduce output below a subsistence level. The fact that Netscape was not allowed access to the most direct, efficient ways to cause the greatest number of consumers to use Navigator is legally irrelevant to a final determination of plaintiffs' §1 claims.

Other courts in similar contexts have declined to find liability where alternative channels of distribution are available to the competitor, even if those channels are not as efficient or reliable as the channels foreclosed by the defendant. In Omega Environmental, Inc. v. Gilbarco, Inc., 127 F.3d 1157 (9th Cir. 1997), for example, the Ninth Circuit found that a manufacturer of petroleum dispensing equipment "foreclosed roughly 38% of the relevant market for sales." 127 F.3d at 1162. Nonetheless, the Court refused to find the defendant liable for exclusive dealing because "potential alternative sources of distribution" existed for its competitors. Id. at 1163. Rejecting plaintiff's argument (similar to the one made in this case) that these alternatives were "inadequate substitutes for the existing distributors," the Court stated that "[c]ompetitors are free to sell directly, to develop alternative distributors, or to compete for the services of existing distributors. Antitrust laws require no more." Id.; accord Seagood Trading Corp. v. Jerrico, Inc., 924 F.2d 1555, 1572-73 (11th Cir. 1991).

Microsoft Corp. ¶312

III. THE STATE LAW CLAIMS

In their amended complaint, the plaintiff states assert that the same facts establishing liability under §§1 and 2 of the Sherman Act mandate a finding of liability under analogous provisions in their own laws. The Court agrees. The facts proving that Microsoft unlawfully maintained its monopoly power in violation of §2 of the Sherman Act are sufficient to meet analogous elements of causes of action arising under the laws of each plaintiff state. The Court reaches the same conclusion with respect to the facts establishing that Microsoft attempted to monopolize the browser market in violation of §2, and with respect to those facts establishing that Microsoft instituted an improper tying arrangement in violation of §1.

The plaintiff states concede that their laws do not condemn any act proved in this case that fails to warrant liability under the Sherman Act. Accordingly, the Court concludes that, for reasons identical to those stated in §II.B, supra, the evidence in this record does not warrant finding Microsoft liable for exclusive dealing under the laws of any of the plaintiff states. . . .

FINAL JUDGMENT
97 F. Supp. 2d 59 (2000)

. . .

1. Divestiture

    a. Not later than four months after entry of this Final Judgment, Microsoft shall submit to the Court and the Plaintiffs a proposed plan of divestiture. The Plaintiffs shall submit any objections to the proposed plan of divestiture to the Court within 60 days of receipt of the plan, and Microsoft shall submit its response within 30 days of receipt of the plaintiffs' objections.

    b. Following approval of a final plan of divestiture by the Court (the "Plan")[1] (and the expiration of the stay pending appeal set forth in section 6.a), Microsoft shall implement such Plan.

    c. The Plan shall provide for the completion, within 12 months of the expiration of the stay pending appeal set forth in section 6.a., of the following steps:

---

[1] Definitions of capitalized terms are set forth in section 7, below.

i. The separation of the Operating Systems Business from the Applications Business, and the transfer of the assets of one of them (the "Separated Business") to a separate entity along with (a) all personnel, systems, and other tangible and intangible assets (including Intellectual Property) used to develop, produce, distribute, market, promote, sell, license and support the products and services of the Separated Business, and (b) such other assets as are necessary to operate the Separated Business as an independent and economically viable entity.

ii. Intellectual Property that is used both in a product developed, distributed, or sold by the Applications Business and in a product developed, distributed, or sold by the Operating Systems Business as of April 27, 2000, shall be assigned to the Applications Business, and the Operating Systems Business shall be granted a perpetual, royalty-free license to license and distribute such Intellectual Property in its products, and, except with respect to such Intellectual Property related to the Internet browser, to develop, license and distribute modified or derivative versions of such Intellectual Property, provided that the Operating Systems Business does not grant rights to such versions to the Applications Business. In the case of such Intellectual Property that is related to the Internet browser, the license shall not grant the Operating Systems Business any right to develop, license, or distribute modified or derivative versions of the Internet browser.

iii. The transfer of ownership of the Separated Business by means of a distribution of stock of the Separated Business to Non-Covered Shareholders of Microsoft, or by other disposition that does not result in a Covered Shareholder owning stock in both the Separated Business and the Remaining Business.

d. Until Implementation of the Plan, Microsoft shall:

i. preserve, maintain, and operate the Operating Systems Business and the Applications Business as ongoing, economically viable businesses, with management, sales, products, and operations of each business held as separate, distinct and apart from one another as they were on April 27, 2000, except to provide the accounting, management, and information services or other necessary support functions provided by Microsoft prior to the entry of this Final Judgment;

ii. use all reasonable efforts to maintain and increase the sales and revenues of both the products produced or sold by the Operating Systems Business and those produced or sold by the Applications Business prior to the Implementation of the Plan and to support research and development and business development efforts of both the Operating Systems Business and the Applications Business;

iii. take no action that undermines, frustrates, interferes with, or makes more difficult the divestiture required by this Final Judgment without the prior approval of the Court; and

iv. file a report with the Court 90 days after entry of this Final Judgment on the steps Microsoft has taken to comply with the requirements of this section 1.d.

2. Provisions Implementing Divestiture

a. After Implementation of the Plan, and throughout the term of this Final Judgment, neither the Operating Systems Business nor the Applications Business, nor any member of their respective Boards of Directors, shall acquire any securities or assets of the other Business; no Covered Shareholder holding securities of either the Operating Systems Business or the Applications Business shall acquire any securities or assets of or shall be an officer, director, or employee of the other Business; and no person who is an officer, director, or employee of the Operating Systems Business or the Applications Business shall be an officer, director, or employee of the other Business.

b. After Implementation of the Plan and throughout the term of this Final Judgment, the Operating Systems Business and the Applications Business shall be prohibited from:

i. merging or otherwise recombining, or entering into any joint venture with one another;

ii. entering into any Agreement with one another under which one of the Businesses develops, sells, licenses for sale or distribution, or

¶312 *Microsoft Corp.*

>> distributes products or services (other than the technologies referred to in the following sentence) developed, sold, licensed, or distributed by the other Business;
>
> iii. providing to the other any APIs, Technical Information, Communications Interfaces, or technical information that is not simultaneously published, disclosed, or made readily available to ISVs, IHVs, and OEMs; and
>
> iv. licensing, selling or otherwise providing to the other Business any product or service on terms more favorable than those available to any similarly situated third party.
>
> Section 2.b.ii shall not prohibit the Operating Systems Business and the Applications Business from licensing technologies (other than Middleware Products) to each other for use in each others' products or services provided that such technology (i) is not and has not been separately sold, licensed, or offered as a product, and (ii) is licensed on terms that are otherwise consistent with this Final Judgment.
>
> c. Three months after Implementation of the Plan and once every three months thereafter throughout the term of this Final Judgment, the Operating Systems Business and the Applications Business shall file with the Plaintiffs a copy of each Agreement (and a memorandum describing each oral Agreement) entered into between them.
>
> d. Throughout the term of this Final Judgment, Microsoft, the Operating Systems Business and the Applications Business shall be prohibited from taking adverse action against any person or entity in whole or in part because such person or entity provided evidence in this case.
>
> e. The obligations and restrictions set forth in sections 3 and 4 herein shall, after the Implementation of the Plan, apply only to the Operating Systems Business.

3. Provisions In Effect Until Full Implementation of the Plan of Divestiture. The provisions in this section 3 shall remain in effect until the earlier of three years after the Implementation of the Plan or the expiration of the term of this Final Judgment.

Microsoft Corp. ¶312

    a.   OEM Relations.

          i.   Ban on Adverse Actions for Supporting Competing Products. Microsoft shall not take or threaten any action adversely affecting any OEM (including but not limited to giving or withholding any consideration such as licensing terms; discounts; technical, marketing, and sales support; enabling programs; product information; technical information; information about future plans; developer tools or developer support; hardware certification; and permission to display trademarks or logos) based directly or indirectly, in whole or in part, on any actual or contemplated action by that OEM:

                (1)   to use, distribute, promote, license, develop, produce or sell any product or service that competes with any Microsoft product or service; or

                (2)   to exercise any of the options or alternatives provided under this Final Judgment.

          ii.   Uniform Terms for Windows Operating System Products Licensed to Covered OEMs. Microsoft shall license Windows Operating System Products to Covered OEMs pursuant to uniform license agreements with uniform terms and conditions and shall not employ market development allowances or discounts in connection with Windows Operating System Products. Without limiting the foregoing, Microsoft shall charge each Covered OEM the applicable royalty for Windows Operating System Products as set forth on a schedule, to be established by Microsoft and published on a Web site accessible to plaintiffs and all Covered OEMs, that provides for uniform royalties for Windows Operating System Products, except that —

                (1)   the schedule may specify different royalties for different language versions, and

                (2)   the schedule may specify reasonable volume discounts based upon actual volume of total shipments of Windows Operating System Products.

Without limiting the foregoing, Microsoft shall afford Covered OEMs equal access to licensing terms; discounts; technical, marketing, and sales support; product information; technical information; information about future plans; developer tools or developer support; hardware certification; and permission to display trademarks or logos. The foregoing requirement insofar as it relates to access to technical information and information about future plans shall not apply to any bona fide joint development effort by Microsoft and a Covered OEM with respect to confidential matters within the scope of that effort. Microsoft shall not terminate a Covered OEM's license for a Windows Operating System Product without having first given the Covered OEM written notice of the reason for the proposed termination and not less than thirty days' opportunity to cure. Microsoft shall not enforce any provision in any Agreement with a Covered OEM that is inconsistent with this Final Judgment.

iii. OEM Flexibility in Product Configuration. Microsoft shall not restrict (by contract or otherwise, including but not limited to granting or withholding consideration) an OEM from modifying the boot sequence, startup folder, internet connection wizard, desktop, preferences, favorites, start page, first screen, or other aspect of a Windows Operating System Product to —

(1) include a registration sequence to obtain subscription or other information from the user;

(2) display icons of or otherwise feature other products or services, regardless of the size or shape of such icons or features, or to remove the icons, folders, start menu entries, or favorites of Microsoft products or services;

(3) display any user interfaces, provided that an icon is also displayed that allows the user to access the Windows user interface; or

(4) launch automatically any non-Microsoft Middleware, Operating System or application, offer its own Internet access provider or other start-up sequence, or offer an option to make non-Microsoft Middleware the Default Middleware and to remove the means of End-User Access for Microsoft's Middleware Product.

Microsoft Corp. ¶312

b. Disclosure of APIs, Communications Interfaces and Technical Information. Microsoft shall disclose to ISVs, IHVs, and OEMs in a Timely Manner, in whatever media Microsoft disseminates such information to its own personnel, all APIs, Technical Information and Communications Interfaces that Microsoft employs to enable —

   i. Microsoft applications to interoperate with Microsoft Platform Software installed on the same Personal Computer, or

   ii. a Microsoft Middleware Product to interoperate with Windows Operating System software (or Middleware distributed with such Operating System) installed on the same Personal Computer, or

   iii. any Microsoft software installed on one computer (including but not limited to server Operating Systems and operating systems for handheld devices) to interoperate with a Windows Operating System (or Middleware distributed with such Operating System) installed on a Personal Computer.

To facilitate compliance, and monitoring of compliance, with the foregoing, Microsoft shall create a secure facility where qualified representatives of OEMs, ISVs, and IHVs shall be permitted to study, interrogate and interact with relevant and necessary portions of the source code and any related documentation of Microsoft Platform Software for the sole purpose of enabling their products to interoperate effectively with Microsoft Platform Software (including exercising any of the options in section 3.a.iii).

c. Knowing Interference with Performance. Microsoft shall not take any action that it knows will interfere with or degrade the performance of any non-Microsoft Middleware when interoperating with any Windows Operating System Product without notifying the supplier of such non-Microsoft Middleware in writing that Microsoft intends to take such action, Microsoft's reasons for taking the action, and any ways known to Microsoft for the supplier to avoid or reduce interference with, or the degrading of, the performance of the supplier's Middleware.

d. Developer Relations. Microsoft shall not take or threaten any action affecting any ISV or IHV (including but not limited to giving or with-

¶312

holding any consideration such as licensing terms; discounts; technical, marketing, and sales support; enabling programs; product information; technical information; information about future plans; developer tools or developer support; hardware certification; and permission to display trademarks or logos) based directly or indirectly, in whole or in part, on any actual or contemplated action by that ISV or IHV to —

    i.   use, distribute, promote or support any Microsoft product or service, or

    ii.   develop, use, distribute, promote or support software that runs on non-Microsoft Middleware or a non-Microsoft Operating System or that competes with any Microsoft product or service, or

    iii.   exercise any of the options or alternatives provided under this Final Judgment.

   e.   Ban on Exclusive Dealing. Microsoft shall not enter into or enforce any Agreement in which a third party agrees, or is offered or granted consideration, to —

    i.   restrict its development, production, distribution, promotion or use of, or payment for, any non-Microsoft Platform Software,

    ii.   distribute, promote or use any Microsoft Platform Software exclusively,

    iii.   degrade the performance of any non-Microsoft Platform Software, or

    iv.   in the case of an agreement with an Internet access provider or Internet content provider, distribute, promote or use Microsoft software in exchange for placement with respect to any aspect of a Windows Operating System Product.

   f.   Ban on Contractual Tying. Microsoft shall not condition the granting of a Windows Operating System Product license, or the terms or administration of such license, on an OEM or other licensee agreeing to license, promote, or distribute any other Microsoft software product that Microsoft distributes separately from the Windows Operating System Product in the retail channel or through Internet access providers, Internet content providers, ISVs or OEMs, whether or not for a separate or positive price.

g. Restriction on Binding Middleware Products to Operating System Products. Microsoft shall not, in any Operating System Product distributed six or more months after the effective date of this Final Judgment, Bind any Middleware Product to a Windows Operating System unless:

i. Microsoft also offers an otherwise identical version of that Operating System Product in which all means of End-User Access to that Middleware Product can readily be removed (a) by OEMs as part of standard OEM preinstallation kits and (b) by end users using add-remove utilities readily accessible in the initial boot process and from the Windows desktop; and

ii. when an OEM removes End-User Access to a Middleware Product from any Personal Computer on which Windows is preinstalled, the royalty paid by that OEM for that copy of Windows is reduced in an amount not less than the product of the otherwise applicable royalty and the ratio of the number of amount in bytes of binary code of (a) the Middleware Product as distributed separately from a Windows Operating System Product to (b) the applicable version of Windows.

h. Agreements Limiting Competition. Microsoft shall not offer, agree to provide, or provide any consideration to any actual or potential Platform Software competitor in exchange for such competitor's agreeing to refrain or refraining in whole or in part from developing, licensing, promoting or distributing any Operating System Product or Middleware Product competitive with any Windows Operating System Product or Middleware Product.

i. Continued Licensing of Predecessor Version. Microsoft shall, when it makes a major Windows Operating System Product release (such as Windows 95, OSR 2.0, OSR 2.5, Windows 98, Windows 2000 Professional, Windows "Millennium," "Whistler," "Blackcomb," and successors to these), continue for three years after said release to license on the same terms and conditions the previous Windows Operating System Product to any OEM that desires such a license. The net royalty rate for

¶312 *Microsoft Corp.*

the previous Windows Operating System Product shall be no more than the average royalty paid by the OEM for such Product prior to the release. The OEM shall be free to market Personal Computers in which it preinstalls such an Operating System Product in the same manner in which it markets Personal Computers preinstalled with other Windows Operating System Products. . . .

7. Definitions

    a. "Agreement" means any agreement, arrangement, alliance, understanding or joint venture, whether written or oral.

    b. "Application Programming Interfaces (APIs)" means the interfaces, service provider interfaces, and protocols that enable a hardware device or an application, Middleware, or server Operating System to obtain services from (or provide services in response to requests from) Platform Software in a Personal Computer and to use, benefit from, and rely on the resources, facilities, and capabilities of such Platform Software.

    c. "Applications Business" means all businesses carried on by Microsoft Corporation on the effective date of this Final Judgment except the Operating Systems Business. Applications Business includes but is not limited to the development, licensing, promotion, and support of client and server applications and Middleware (e.g., Office, BackOffice, Internet Information Server, SQL Server, etc.), Internet Explorer, Mobile Explorer and other Web browsers, Streaming Audio and Video client and server software, transaction server software, SNA server software, indexing server software, XML servers and parsers, Microsoft Management Server, Java virtual machines, Frontpage Express (and other Web authoring tools), Outlook Express (and other e-mail clients), Media player, voice recognition software, Net Meeting (and other collaboration software), developer tools, hardware, MSN, MSNBC, Slate, Expedia, and all investments owned by Microsoft in partners or joint venturers, or in ISVs, IHVs, OEMs or other distributors, developers, and promoters of Microsoft products, or in other information technology or communications businesses.

    d. "Bind" means to include a product in an Operating System Product in such a way that either an OEM or an end user cannot readily remove or uninstall the product.

e. "Business" means the Operating Systems Business or the Applications Business.

f. "Communications Interfaces" means the interfaces and protocols that enable software installed on other computers (including servers and handheld devices) to interoperate with the Microsoft Platform Software on a Personal Computer.

g. "Covered OEM" means one of the 20 OEMs with the highest volume of licenses of Windows Operating System Products from Microsoft in the calendar year preceding the effective date of the Final Judgment. At the beginning of each year, starting on January 1, 2002, Microsoft shall redetermine the Covered OEMs for the new calendar year, based on sales volume during the preceding calendar year.

h. "Covered Shareholder" means a shareholder of Microsoft on the date of entry of this Final Judgment who is a present or former employee, officer or director of Microsoft and who owns directly or beneficially more than 5 percent of the voting stock of the firm.

i. "Default Middleware" means Middleware configured to launch automatically (that is, by "default") to provide particular functionality when other Middleware has not been selected for this purpose. For example, a default browser is Middleware configured to launch automatically to display Web pages transmitted over the Internet or an intranet that bear the .htm extension, when other software has not been selected for this purpose.

j. "End-User Access" means the invocation of Middleware directly or indirectly by an end user of a Personal Computer or the ability of such an end user to invoke Middleware. "End-User Access" includes invocation of Middleware by end users which is compelled by the design of the Operating System Product.

k. "IHV" means an independent hardware vendor that develops hardware to be included in or used with a Personal Computer.

¶312 *Microsoft Corp.*

l. "Implementation of the Plan" means full completion of all of the steps described in section 1.c.

m. "Intellectual Property" means copyrights, patents, trademarks and trade secrets used by Microsoft or licensed by Microsoft to third parties.

n. "ISV" means any entity other than Microsoft (or any subsidiary, division, or other operating unit of any such other entity) that is engaged in the development and licensing (or other marketing) of software products intended to interoperate with Microsoft Platform Software.

o. "Manager" means a Microsoft employee who is responsible for the direct or indirect supervision of more than 100 other employees.

p. "Microsoft" means Microsoft Corporation, the Separated Business, the Remaining Business, their successors and assigns (including any transferee or assignee of any ownership rights to, control of, or ability to license the patents referred to in this Final Judgment), their subsidiaries, affiliates, directors, officers, managers, agents, and employees, and all other persons in active concert or participation with any of them who shall have received actual notice of this Final Judgment by personal service or otherwise.

q. "Middleware" means software that operates, directly or through other software, between an Operating System and another type of software (such as an application, a server Operating System, or a database management system) by offering services via APIs or Communications Interfaces to such other software, and could, if ported to or interoperable with multiple Operating Systems, enable software products written for that Middleware to be run on multiple Operating System Products. Examples of Middleware within the meaning of this Final Judgment include Internet browsers, e-mail client software, multimedia viewing software, Office, and the Java Virtual Machine. Examples of software that are not Middleware within the meaning of this Final Judgment are disk compression and memory management.

Microsoft Corp. ¶312

r. "Middleware Product" means

   i. Internet browsers, e-mail client software, multimedia viewing software, instant messaging software, and voice recognition software, or

   ii. software distributed by Microsoft that —

   (1) is, or has in the applicable preceding year been, distributed separately from an Operating System Product in the retail channel or through Internet access providers, Internet content providers, ISVs or OEMs, and

   (2) provides functionality similar to that provided by Middleware offered by a competitor to Microsoft.

s. "Non-Covered Shareholder" means a shareholder of Microsoft on the record date for the transaction that effects the transfer of ownership of the Separated Business under Section 1.c.iii who is not a Covered Shareholder on the date of entry of this Final Judgment.

t. "OEM" means the manufacturer or assembler of a personal computer.

u. "Operating System" means the software that controls the allocation and usage of hardware resources (such as memory, central processing unit time, disk space, and peripheral devices) of a computer, providing a "platform" by exposing APIs that applications use to "call upon" the Operating System's underlying software routines in order to perform functions.

v. "Operating System Product" means an Operating System and additional software shipped with the Operating System, whether or not such additional software is marketed for a positive price. An Operating System Product includes Operating System Product upgrades that may be distributed separately from the Operating System Product.

w. "Operating Systems Business" means the development, licensing, promotion, and support of Operating System Products for computing devices including but not limited to (i) Personal Computers, (ii) other computers based on Intel x86 or competitive microprocessors, such as servers, (iii) handheld devices such as personal digital assistants and cellular telephones, and (iv) television set-top boxes.

x. "Personal Computer" means any computer configured so that its primary purpose is to be used by one person at a time, that uses a video display and keyboard (whether or not the video display and keyboard are actually included), and that contains an Intel x86, successor, or competitive microprocessor, and computers that are commercial substitutes for such computers.

y. "Plaintiff" means the United States or any of the plaintiff States in this action.

z. "Plan" means the final plan of divestiture approved by the Court.

aa. "Platform Software" means an Operating System or Middleware or a combination of an Operating System and Middleware.

bb. "Remaining Business" means whichever of the Operating Systems Business and the Applications Businesses is not transferred to a separate entity pursuant to the Plan.

cc. "Separated Business" means whichever of the Operating Systems Business and the Applications Businesses is transferred to a separate entity pursuant to the Plan.

dd. "Technical Information" means all information regarding the identification and means of using APIs and Communications Interfaces that competent software developers require to make their products running on any computer interoperate effectively with Microsoft Platform Software running on a Personal Computer. Technical information includes but is not limited to reference implementations, communications protocols, file formats, data formats, syntaxes and grammars, data structure definitions and layouts, error codes, memory allocation and deallocation conventions, threading and synchronization conventions, functional specifications and descriptions, algorithms for data translation or reformatting (including compression/decompression algorithms and encryption/decryption algorithms), registry settings, and field contents.

Microsoft Corp. ¶312

ee. "Timely Manner": disclosure of APIs, Technical Information and Communications Interfaces in a timely manner means, at a minimum, publication on a Web site accessible by ISVs, IHVs, and OEMs at the earliest of the time that such APIs, Technical Information, or Communications Interfaces are (1) disclosed to Microsoft's applications developers, (2) used by Microsoft's own Platform Software developers in software released by Microsoft in alpha, beta, release candidate, final or other form, (3) disclosed to any third party, or (4) within 90 days of a final release of a Windows Operating System Product, no less than 5 days after a material change is made between the most recent beta or release candidate version and the final release.

ff. "Windows Operating System Product" means software code (including source code and binary code, and any other form in which Microsoft distributes its Windows Operating Systems for Personal Computers) of Windows 95, Windows 98, Windows 2000 Professional, and their successors, including the Windows Operating Systems for Personal Computers codenamed "Millennium," "Whistler," and "Blackcomb," and their successors.

¶313 *Intel Corp.*

Page 477. After ¶313, add the following:

IN RE INTEL CORP.
F.T.C. Docket No. 9288 (1999)

Analysis of Proposed Consent Order to Aid Public Comment

The Federal Trade Commission has accepted for public comment an Agreement Containing Consent Order with Intel Corporation ("Intel") to resolve the matters charged in an administrative Complaint issued by the Commission on June 8, 1998. The Agreement has been placed on the public record for sixty (60) days for receipt of comments from interested members of the public. The Agreement is for settlement purposes only and does not constitute an admission by Intel that the law has been violated as alleged in the Complaint or that the facts alleged in the Complaint, other than jurisdictional facts, are true. [On August 6, 1999, the FTC voted to approve the consent order described herein.]

I. The Complaint

The Complaint alleges that Intel has monopoly power in the worldwide market for general purpose microprocessors. According to the Complaint, Intel's market dominance is reflected in a market share approximating 80 percent of dollar sales, together with high entry barriers including large sunk costs of design and manufacture, substantial economies of scale, customers' investments in existing software, the need to attract support from software developers, and reputational barriers.

The Complaint alleges that Intel sought to maintain its dominance by, among other things, denying advance technical information and product samples of microprocessors to Intel customers ("original equipment manufacturers" or "OEMs") and threatening to withhold product from those OEMs as a means of coercing those customers into licensing their patented innovations to Intel.

A microprocessor is an integrated circuit that serves as the central processing unit (or CPU) of computer systems. Microprocessors are sometimes described as the "brains" of computers because they perform the major data processing functions essential to computer systems. Advance technical information about new microprocessor products is essential to Intel's OEM customers, who design, develop, manufacture, and sell computer system products

Intel Corp. ¶313

such as servers, workstations, and desktop and mobile personal computers. Computer design and development require the effective integration of multiple complex microelectronics components (including microprocessors, memory components, core logic chips, graphics controllers, and various input and output devices) into a coherent system. To achieve such system integration, a computer OEM requires product specifications and other technical information about each component, such as the electrical, mechanical, and thermal characteristics of the microprocessor. OEMs also need advance product samples, errata, and related technical assistance in order to perform system testing and debugging, thereby assuring the high performance and reliability of new computer products.

Intel promotes and markets its microprocessors by providing customers with technical information about new Intel products in advance of their commercial release, subject to formal nondisclosure agreements. Such information sharing has substantial commercial benefits for Intel and its OEM customers. Customers benefit because the information enables them to develop and introduce new computer system products incorporating the latest microprocessors as early and efficiently as possible. Intel benefits because a larger group of OEMs can sell new computer systems incorporating Intel's newest microprocessors as soon as the new microprocessors are introduced to the market.

The Complaint charges that Intel suspended its traditional commercial relationships with three established customers—Digital Equipment Corporation, Intergraph Corporation, and Compaq Computer Corporation—by refusing to provide advance technical information about, and product samples of, Intel microprocessors. Intel did so, according to the Complaint, to force those customers to end disputes with Intel concerning the customers' asserted intellectual property rights and to grant Intel licenses to patented technology developed and owned by those customers. In at least one of the cases, the Complaint alleges that Intel also acted to create uncertainty in the marketplace about the customer's future source of supply of Intel microprocessors.

The computer industry is characterized by short, dynamic product cycles, which are generally measured in months. Time to market is crucial. Indeed, the denial of advance product information is virtually tantamount to a denial of actual parts, because an OEM customer lacking such information simply cannot design new computer systems on a competitive schedule with other OEMs. An OEM who suffers denial of such information over a period of months will lose much of the profits it might otherwise have earned even from a successful new computer model. Continued denial of advance technical information to an OEM by a dominant supplier can make a customer's very

¶313 *Intel Corp.*

existence as an OEM untenable.

As a result of the commercial pressure exerted by Intel's conduct, Compaq and Digital quickly entered into cross-license arrangements with Intel. Intergraph was able to resist that pressure because it succeeded in obtaining a preliminary injunction from a federal district court requiring Intel to resume and continue supplying Intergraph with advance product information, part samples, and other technical support pending a judicial resolution on the merits of the claims in the lawsuit.

The alleged conduct tends to reinforce Intel's domination of the general purpose microprocessor market in at least three ways. First, the alleged conduct tends to give Intel preferential access to a wide range of technologies being developed by many other firms in the industry. To the extent that firms desiring to compete with Intel are unable to obtain comparable access to such a wide range of technology, they can be seriously disadvantaged, thus making it more difficult for them to challenge Intel's dominance. Second, because patent rights are an important means of promoting innovation, coercion that forces customers to license away rights to microprocessor-related technologies on unfavorable terms tends to diminish the customers' incentives to develop such technologies, and thus harms competition by reducing innovation. Finally, Intel's conduct tends to make it more difficult for an OEM to serve as a platform for microprocessors that compete with Intel's. Intel's actions ensure that Intel can act as a conduit for technology flows from one OEM to another. That is, an OEM that seeks to enforce its intellectual property rights against other Intel customers may face retaliation from Intel, as the Complaint alleges Compaq did when it sued Packard-Bell for patent infringement. The result is that OEMs find it more difficult to differentiate their computer systems from their competitors through patented technology. As a result, an OEM seeking to use non-Intel microprocessors is less able to offset the lack of an Intel microprocessor by the strength of its own reputation for offering superior technology in other areas. For all of these reasons, continuation of this pattern of conduct would likely have injured competition by entrenching Intel's dominant position. The Complaint also alleges that Intel's exclusionary conduct was not reasonably necessary to serve any legitimate, procompetitive purpose.

Exclusionary conduct by a monopolist that is reasonably capable of significantly contributing to the maintenance of a firm's dominance through unjustified means has long been understood to give rise to serious competitive concerns. See, e.g., *Lorain Journal*; *Aspen*; *Grinnell*; *Barry Wright*.

Such conduct harms consumers, not only because competition brings

Intel Corp. ¶313

lower prices, but also because competition is a powerful spur to the development of new, better, and more diverse products and processes. Unjustified conduct by a monopolist that removes the incentive to such competition by depriving innovators of their reward or otherwise tilting the playing field against new entrants or fringe competitors thus has a direct and substantial impact upon future consumers.

In the absence of a legitimate business justification that outweighs these concerns, such conduct constitutes a violation of Section 2 of the Sherman Act and therefore Section 5 of the Federal Trade Commission Act. In issuing the Complaint, the Commission found reason to believe that such a violation had occurred.

II. Terms of the Proposed Consent Order

The Proposed Order would remedy all of the concerns embodied in the Complaint. The substantive prohibition, Section II.A, prohibits Intel from withholding or threatening to withhold certain advance technical information from a customer or taking other specified actions with respect to such information for reasons relating to an intellectual property dispute with that customer. It also prohibits Intel from refusing or threatening to refuse to sell microprocessors to a customer for reasons related to an intellectual property dispute with that customer. This provision is designed to prevent Intel from restricting access to microprocessor products, or advance technical information relating to such products, as leverage in an intellectual property dispute against a customer that is receiving advance technical information from Intel at the time the dispute arises. The Proposed Order does not impose any kind of broad "compulsory licensing" regime upon Intel. So long as it is otherwise lawful, Intel is free to decide in the first instance whether it chooses to provide or not provide information to customers, and whether to provide more information or earlier information to specific customers in furtherance of a joint venture or other legitimate activity. Moreover, the Order is limited to the types of information that Intel routinely gives to customers to enable them to use Intel microprocessors, not information that would be used to design or manufacture microprocessors in competition with Intel.

In short, Paragraph II.A. secures to Intel customers the right to seek full and fair value for their intellectual property, free from the risk of curtailment of needed advance technical information or product. With one exception, Intel will be required to continue providing information and product while the customer seeks any of a range of legal and equitable remedies available to it, such as damages (trebled or otherwise increased in appropriate cases), reason-

¶313

Intel Corp.

able royalties, and attorneys fees and costs. These remedies will generally be sufficient to protect the customer in its exercise of its intellectual property rights.

The exception involves situations where a customer maintains the right to seek an injunction against Intel's manufacture, use, sale, offer to sell or importation of its microprocessors. The Order contemplates that Intel may request a customer to waive that remedy and give the customer a reasonable opportunity to make a simple written statement to that effect. If the customer refuses, Intel will not be required by this Order to continue providing information or product with respect to the microprocessors that the customer is seeking to enjoin. This part of the Order strikes an appropriate balance, on a prospective basis, between the interests of Intel and its customers. If a customer chooses to seek an injunction against Intel's microprocessors, it cannot, under the provisions of this Order, be assured of continuing to receive advance technical information about the very same microprocessors that it is attempting to enjoin. If an Intel customer nevertheless wishes to seek injunctive relief against Intel's manufacture, use, sale, offer to sell or importation, it remains free to do so, but without the protections in this Order. In all other circumstances, Intel is required to continue supplying technical information and product under the Proposed Order. . . .[*]

---

[*]The complete Decision and Order can be found at http://www.ftc.gov/os/1999/9908/inteld%26o.htm, and a complete version of the analysis excerpted in the text can be found at http://www.ftc.gov/os/1999/9903/d09288intelanalysis.htm.

Chapter 4

Vertical Restraints

4A. Restricted Distribution

Page 637. After ¶407, add the following:

STATE OIL CO. v. KHAN
522 U.S. 3 (1997)

Justice O'CONNOR. . . . Under §1 of the Sherman Act, "[e]very contract, combination . . . , or conspiracy, in restraint of trade" is illegal. In *Albrecht*, this Court held that vertical maximum price fixing is a per se violation of that statute. In this case, we are asked to reconsider that decision in light of subsequent decisions of this Court. We conclude that *Albrecht* should be overruled.

I

Respondents, Barkat U. Khan and his corporation, entered into an agreement with petitioner, State Oil Company, to lease and operate a gas station and convenience store owned by State Oil. The agreement provided that respondents would obtain the station's gasoline supply from State Oil at a price equal to a suggested retail price set by State Oil, less a margin of 3.25 cents per gallon. Under the agreement, respondents could charge any amount for gasoline sold to the station's customers, but if the price charged was higher than State Oil's suggested retail price, the excess was to be rebated to State Oil. Respondents could sell gasoline for less than State Oil's suggested retail price, but any such decrease would reduce their 3.25 cents-per-gallon margin.

About a year after respondents began operating the gas station, they fell behind in lease payments. State Oil then gave notice of its intent to terminate the agreement and commenced a state court proceeding to evict respondents. At State Oil's request, the state court appointed a receiver to operate the gas

75

station. The receiver operated the station for several months without being subject to the price restraints in respondents' agreement with State Oil. According to respondents, the receiver obtained an overall profit margin in excess of 3.25 cents per gallon by lowering the price of regular-grade gasoline and raising the price of premium grades.

Respondents sued State Oil in the United States District Court for the Northern District of Illinois, alleging in part that State Oil had engaged in price fixing in violation of §1 of the Sherman Act by preventing respondents from raising or lowering retail gas prices. According to the complaint, but for the agreement with State Oil, respondents could have charged different prices based on the grades of gasoline, in the same way that the receiver had, thereby achieving increased sales and profits. State Oil responded that the agreement did not actually prevent respondents from setting gasoline prices, and that, in substance, respondents did not allege a violation of antitrust laws by their claim that State Oil's suggested retail price was not optimal.

The District Court found that the allegations in the complaint did not state a per se violation of the Sherman Act because they did not establish the sort of "manifestly anticompetitive implications or pernicious effect on competition" that would justify per se prohibition of State Oil's conduct. Subsequently, in ruling on cross-motions for summary judgment, the District Court concluded that respondents had failed to demonstrate antitrust injury or harm to competition. The District Court held that respondents had not shown that a difference in gasoline pricing would have increased the station's sales; nor had they shown that State Oil had market power or that its pricing provisions affected competition in a relevant market. Accordingly, the District Court entered summary judgment for State Oil on respondents' Sherman Act claim.

The Court of Appeals for the Seventh Circuit reversed. The court first noted that the agreement between respondents and State Oil did indeed fix maximum gasoline prices by making it "worthless" for respondents to exceed the suggested retail prices. After reviewing legal and economic aspects of price fixing, the court concluded that State Oil's pricing scheme was a per se antitrust violation under *Albrecht*. Although the Court of Appeals characterized *Albrecht* as "unsound when decided" and "inconsistent with later decisions" of this Court, it felt constrained to follow that decision. In light of *Albrecht* and *ARCO*, the court found that respondents could have suffered antitrust injury from not being able to adjust gasoline prices.

We granted certiorari to consider two questions, whether State Oil's conduct constitutes a per se violation of the Sherman Act and whether respondents are entitled to recover damages based on that conduct.

Khan ¶407

II

A

Although the Sherman Act, by its terms, prohibits every agreement "in restraint of trade," this Court has long recognized that Congress intended to outlaw only unreasonable restraints. See, e.g., *Maricopa* (citing *Joint Traffic*). As a consequence, most antitrust claims are analyzed under a "rule of reason," according to which the finder of fact must decide whether the questioned practice imposes an unreasonable restraint on competition, taking into account a variety of factors, including specific information about the relevant business, its condition before and after the restraint was imposed, and the restraint's history, nature, and effect. See *Maricopa* (citing *Chicago Board of Trade*).

Some types of restraints, however, have such predictable and pernicious anticompetitive effect, and such limited potential for procompetitive benefit, that they are deemed unlawful per se. *Northern Pacific*. Per se treatment is appropriate "[o]nce experience with a particular kind of restraint enables the Court to predict with confidence that the rule of reason will condemn it." *Maricopa*; see also *Broadcast Music*. Thus, we have expressed reluctance to adopt per se rules with regard to "restraints imposed in the context of business relationships where the economic impact of certain practices is not immediately obvious." *Indiana Dentists*.

A review of this Court's decisions leading up to and beyond *Albrecht* is relevant to our assessment of the continuing validity of the per se rule established in *Albrecht*. Beginning with *Dr. Miles*, the Court recognized the illegality of agreements under which manufacturers or suppliers set the minimum resale prices to be charged by their distributors. By 1940, the Court broadly declared all business combinations "formed for the purpose and with the effect of raising, depressing, fixing, pegging, or stabilizing the price of a commodity in interstate or foreign commerce" illegal per se. *Socony*. Accordingly, the Court condemned an agreement between two affiliated liquor distillers to limit the maximum price charged by retailers in Kiefer-Stewart Co. v. Joseph E. Seagram & Sons, 340 U.S. 211 (1951), noting that agreements to fix maximum prices, "no less than those to fix minimum prices, cripple the freedom of traders and thereby restrain their ability to sell in accordance with their own judgment."

In subsequent cases, the Court's attention turned to arrangements through which suppliers imposed restrictions on dealers with respect to matters other than resale price. In White Motor Co. v. United States, 372 U.S. 253 (1963), the Court considered the validity of a manufacturer's assignment of exclusive territories to its distributors and dealers. The Court determined that too little was known about the competitive impact of such vertical limitations to warrant treating them as per se unlawful. Four years later, in United States v. Arnold, Schwinn & Co., 388 U.S. 365 (1967), the Court reconsidered the status of exclusive dealer territories and held that, upon the transfer of title to goods to a distributor, a supplier's imposition of territorial restrictions on the distributor was "so obviously destructive of competition" as to constitute a per se violation of the Sherman Act. In Schwinn, the Court acknowledged that some vertical restrictions, such as the conferral of territorial rights or franchises, could have procompetitive benefits by allowing smaller enterprises to compete, and that such restrictions might avert vertical integration in the distribution process. The Court drew the line, however, at permitting manufacturers to control product marketing once dominion over the goods had passed to dealers.

Albrecht, decided the following Term, involved a newspaper publisher who had granted exclusive territories to independent carriers subject to their adherence to a maximum price on resale of the newspapers to the public. Influenced by its decisions in *Socony*, *Kiefer-Stewart*, and *Schwinn*, the Court concluded that it was per se unlawful for the publisher to fix the maximum resale price of its newspapers. The Court acknowledged that "[m]aximum and minimum price fixing may have different consequences in many situations," but nonetheless condemned maximum price fixing for "substituting the perhaps erroneous judgment of a seller for the forces of the competitive market."

Albrecht was animated in part by the fear that vertical maximum price fixing could allow suppliers to discriminate against certain dealers, restrict the services that dealers could afford to offer customers, or disguise minimum price fixing schemes. The Court rejected the notion (both on the record of that case and in the abstract) that, because the newspaper publisher "granted exclusive territories, a price ceiling was necessary to protect the public from price gouging by dealers who had monopoly power in their own territories."

In a vigorous dissent, Justice Harlan asserted that the majority had erred in equating the effects of maximum and minimum price fixing. Justice Harlan pointed out that, because the majority was establishing a per se rule, the proper inquiry was "not whether dictation of maximum prices is ever illegal, but whether it is always illegal." He also faulted the majority for conclusively listing "certain unfortunate consequences that maximum price dictation might have in other cases," even as it rejected evidence that the publisher's practice of fixing maximum prices counteracted potentially anticompetitive actions by its distributors. Justice Stewart also dissented, asserting that the publisher's maximum price fixing scheme should be properly viewed as promoting competition, because it protected consumers from dealers such as Albrecht, who, as "the only person who could sell for home delivery the city's only daily morning newspaper," was "a monopolist within his own territory."

Nine years later, in *Sylvania*, the Court overruled *Schwinn*, thereby rejecting application of a per se rule in the context of vertical nonprice restrictions. The Court acknowledged the principle of stare decisis, but explained that the need for clarification in the law justified reconsideration of *Schwinn*. . . .

In *Sylvania*, the Court declined to comment on *Albrecht*'s per se treatment of vertical maximum price restrictions, noting that the issue "involve[d] significantly different questions of analysis and policy." Subsequent decisions of the Court, however, have hinted that the analytical underpinnings of *Albrecht* were substantially weakened by *Sylvania*. We noted in *Maricopa* that vertical restraints are generally more defensible than horizontal restraints. And we explained in 324 Liquor Corp. v. Duffy, 479 U.S. 335 (1987), that decisions such as *Sylvania* "recognize the possibility that a vertical restraint imposed by a single manufacturer or wholesaler may stimulate interbrand competition even as it reduces intrabrand competition."

Most recently, in *ARCO*, although *Albrecht*'s continuing validity was not squarely before the Court, some disfavor with that decision was signaled by our statement that we would "assume, arguendo, that *Albrecht* correctly held that vertical, maximum price fixing is subject to the per se rule." More significantly, we specifically acknowledged that vertical maximum price fixing "may have procompetitive interbrand effects," and pointed out that, in the wake of *Sylvania*, "[t]he procompetitive potential of a vertical maximum price restraint is more evident . . . than it was when *Albrecht* was decided, because exclusive territorial arrangements and other nonprice restrictions were unlawful per se in 1968." 495 U.S., at 344 n.13 (citing several commentators identifying procompetitive effects of vertical maximum price fixing . . .).

B

Thus, our reconsideration of *Albrecht*'s continuing validity is informed by several of our decisions, as well as a considerable body of scholarship discussing the effects of vertical restraints. Our analysis is also guided by our general view that the primary purpose of the antitrust laws is to protect interbrand competition. See, e.g., *Business Electronics*. "Low prices," we have explained, "benefit consumers regardless of how those prices are set, and so long as they are above predatory levels, they do not threaten competition." *ARCO*. Our interpretation of the Sherman Act also incorporates the notion that condemnation of practices resulting in lower prices to consumers is "especially costly" because "cutting prices in order to increase business often is the very essence of competition." *Matsushita*.

So informed, we find it difficult to maintain that vertically-imposed maximum prices could harm consumers or competition to the extent necessary to justify their per se invalidation. As Chief Judge Posner wrote for the Court of Appeals in this case:

> "As for maximum resale price fixing, unless the supplier is a monopolist he cannot squeeze his dealers' margins below a competitive level; the attempt to do so would just drive the dealers into the arms of a competing supplier. A supplier might, however, fix a maximum resale price in order to prevent his dealers from exploiting a monopoly position.... [S]uppose that State Oil, perhaps to encourage ... dealer services ... has spaced its dealers sufficiently far apart to limit competition among them (or even given each of them an exclusive territory); and suppose further that Union 76 is a sufficiently distinctive and popular brand to give the dealers in it at least a modicum of monopoly power. Then State Oil might want to place a ceiling on the dealers' resale prices in order to prevent them from exploiting that monopoly power fully. It would do this not out of disinterested malice, but in its commercial self-interest. The higher the price at which gasoline is resold, the smaller the volume sold, and so the lower the profit to the supplier if the higher profit per gallon at the higher price is being snared by the dealer."

See also R. Bork, The Antitrust Paradox 281-282 (1978) ("There could, of course, be no anticonsumer effect from [the type of price fixing considered in *Albrecht*], and one suspects that the paper has a legitimate interest in keeping subscriber prices down in order to increase circulation and maximize revenues from advertising").

We recognize that the *Albrecht* decision presented a number of theoretical justifications for a per se rule against vertical maximum price fixing. But criticism of those premises abounds. The *Albrecht* decision was grounded in the fear that maximum price fixing by suppliers could interfere with dealer freedom. In response, as one commentator has pointed out, "the ban on maximum resale price limitations declared in *Albrecht* in the name of 'dealer freedom' has actually prompted many suppliers to integrate forward into distribution, thus eliminating the very independent trader for whom *Albrecht* professed solicitude." 7 P. Areeda, Antitrust Law, ¶1635, p. 395 (1989). For example, integration in the newspaper industry since *Albrecht* has given rise to litigation between independent distributors and publishers. See P. Areeda & H. Hovenkamp, Antitrust Law ¶729.7, pp. 599-614 (1996 Supp.).

The *Albrecht* Court also expressed the concern that maximum prices may be set too low for dealers to offer consumers essential or desired services. But such conduct, by driving away customers, would seem likely to harm manufacturers as well as dealers and consumers, making it unlikely that a supplier would set such a price as a matter of business judgment. See, e.g., Lopatka, Stephen Breyer and Modern Antitrust: A Snug Fit, 40 Antitrust Bull. 1, 60 (1995); Blair & Lang, *Albrecht* After *ARCO*: Maximum Resale Price Fixing Moves Toward the Rule of Reason, 44 Vand. L. Rev. 1007, 1034 (1991). In addition, *Albrecht* noted that vertical maximum price fixing could effectively channel distribution through large or specially-advantaged dealers. It is unclear, however, that a supplier would profit from limiting its market by excluding potential dealers. See, e.g., Easterbrook, supra, at 905-908. Further, although vertical maximum price fixing might limit the viability of inefficient dealers, that consequence is not necessarily harmful to competition and consumers. See, e.g., Easterbrook, supra, at 907; Lopatka, supra, at 60.

Finally, *Albrecht* reflected the Court's fear that maximum price fixing could be used to disguise arrangements to fix minimum prices, which remain illegal per se. Although we have acknowledged the possibility that maximum pricing might mask minimum pricing, see *Maricopa*, we believe that such conduct as with the other concerns articulated in *Albrecht* can be appropriately recognized and punished under the rule of reason. See, e.g., Easterbrook, 48 U. Chi. L. Rev., at 901-904; see also Pitofsky, In Defense of Discounters: The No-Frills Case for a Per se Rule Against Vertical Price Fixing, 71 Geo. L.J. 1487, 1490, n. 17 (1983).

Not only are the potential injuries cited in *Albrecht* less serious than the Court imagined, the per se rule established therein could in fact exacerbate problems related to the unrestrained exercise of market power by monopolist-dealers. Indeed, both courts and antitrust scholars have noted that *Albrecht*'s rule may actually harm consumers and manufacturers. See, e.g., Caribe BMW v. Bayerische Motoren Werke Aktiengesellschaft, 19 F.3d 745, 753 (C.A.1 1994) (Breyer, C.J.); Areeda, *supra*, ¶1636a, at 395; G. Mathewson & R. Winter, Competition Policy and Vertical Exchange 13-14 (1985). Other commentators have also explained that *Albrecht*'s per se rule has even more potential for deleterious effect on competition after our decision in *Sylvania*, because, now that vertical nonprice restrictions are not unlawful per se, the likelihood of dealer monopoly power is increased. See, e.g., Easterbrook, supra, at 890, n. 20; see also *ARCO*. We do not intend to suggest that dealers generally possess sufficient market power to exploit a monopoly situation. Such retail market power may in fact be uncommon. See, e.g., *Business Electronics* and *Sylvania*. Nor do we hold that a ban on vertical maximum price fixing inevitably has anticompetitive consequences in the exclusive dealer context.

After reconsidering *Albrecht*'s rationale and the substantial criticism the decision has received, however, we conclude that there is insufficient economic justification for per se invalidation of vertical maximum price fixing. That is so not only because it is difficult to accept the assumptions underlying *Albrecht*, but also because *Albrecht* has little or no relevance to ongoing enforcement of the Sherman Act. See *Copperweld*. Moreover, neither the parties nor any of the amici curiae have called our attention to any cases in which enforcement efforts have been directed solely against the conduct encompassed by *Albrecht*'s per se rule.

Respondents argue that reconsideration of *Albrecht* should require "persuasive, expert testimony establishing that the per se rule has distorted the market." Their reasoning ignores the fact that *Albrecht* itself relied solely upon hypothetical effects of vertical maximum price fixing. Further, *Albrecht*'s dire predictions have not been borne out, even though manufacturers and suppliers appear to have fashioned schemes to get around the per se rule against vertical maximum price fixing. In these circumstances, it is the retention of the rule of *Albrecht*, and not, as respondents would have it, the rule's elimination, that lacks adequate justification. See, e.g., *Sylvania*. . . .

C

Despite what Chief Judge Posner aptly described as *Albrecht*'s "infirmities, [and] its increasingly wobbly, moth-eaten foundations," there remains the question whether *Albrecht* deserves continuing respect under the doctrine of stare decisis. The Court of Appeals was correct in applying that principle despite disagreement with *Albrecht*, for it is this Court's prerogative alone to overrule one of its precedents.

We approach the reconsideration of decisions of this Court with the utmost caution. Stare decisis reflects "a policy judgment that 'in most matters it is more important that the applicable rule of law be settled than that it be settled right.'" Agostini v. Felton, 521 U.S. 203, 235 (1997) (quoting Burnet v. Coronado Oil & Gas Co., 285 U.S. 393 (1932) (Brandeis, J., dissenting)). It "is the preferred course because it promotes the evenhanded, predictable, and consistent development of legal principles, fosters reliance on judicial decisions, and contributes to the actual and perceived integrity of the judicial process." Payne v. Tennessee, 501 U.S. 808 (1991). This Court has expressed its reluctance to overrule decisions involving statutory interpretation, see, e.g., Illinois Brick Co. v. Illinois, 431 U.S. 720 (1977), and has acknowledged that stare decisis concerns are at their acme in cases involving property and contract rights, see, e.g., *Payne*, 501 U.S., at 828. Both of those concerns are arguably relevant in this case.

But "[s]tare decisis is not an inexorable command." Ibid. In the area of antitrust law, there is a competing interest, well-represented in this Court's decisions, in recognizing and adapting to changed circumstances and the lessons of accumulated experience. Thus, the general presumption that legislative changes should be left to Congress has less force with respect to the Sherman Act in light of the accepted view that Congress "expected the courts to give shape to the statute's broad mandate by drawing on common-law tradition." *Engineers*. As we have explained, the term "restraint of trade," as used in § 1, also "invokes the common law itself, and not merely the static content that the common law had assigned to the term in 1890." *Business Electronics*; see also *Sylvania*; McNally v. United States, 483 U.S. 350, 372-373 (1987) (Stevens, J. dissenting). Accordingly, this Court has reconsidered its decisions construing the Sherman Act when the theoretical underpinnings of those decisions are called into serious question. See, e.g., *Copperweld*; *Sylvania*; Tigner v. Texas, 310 U.S. 141 (1940).

Although we do not "lightly assume that the economic realities underlying earlier decisions have changed, or that earlier judicial perceptions of those realities were in error," we have noted that "different sorts of agreements" may amount to restraints of trade "in varying times and circumstances," and "[i]t would make no sense to create out of the single term 'restraint of trade' a chronologically schizoid statute, in which a 'rule of reason' evolves with new circumstances and new wisdom, but a line of per se illegality remains forever fixed where it was." *Business Electronics*. Just as *Schwinn* was "the subject of continuing controversy and confusion" under the "great weight" of scholarly criticism, *Sylvania*, *Albrecht* has been widely criticized since its inception. With the views underlying *Albrecht* eroded by this Court's precedent, there is not much of that decision to salvage. See, e.g., Neal v. United States, 516 U.S. 284 (1996); Patterson v. McLean Credit Union, 491 U.S. 164 (1989); Rodriguez de Quijas v. Shearson/American Express, 490 U.S. 477, 480-481 (1989).

Although the rule of *Albrecht* has been in effect for some time, the inquiry we must undertake requires considering "'the effect of the antitrust laws upon vertical distributional restraints in the American economy today.'" *Sylvania* (quoting *Schwinn* (Stewart, J., concurring in part and dissenting in part)). As the Court noted in *ARCO*, there has not been another case since *Albrecht* in which this Court has "confronted an unadulterated vertical, maximum-price-fixing arrangement." Now that we confront *Albrecht* directly, we find its conceptual foundations gravely weakened.

In overruling *Albrecht*, we of course do not hold that all vertical maximum price fixing is per se lawful. Instead, vertical maximum price fixing, like the majority of commercial arrangements subject to the antitrust laws, should be evaluated under the rule of reason. In our view, rule-of-reason analysis will effectively identify those situations in which vertical maximum price fixing amounts to anticompetitive conduct. . . .[*]

---

[*] On remand, the plaintiff chose not to argue that the maximum price was unreasonable but instead claimed that the arrangement constituted minimum price fixing, an argument the court rejected. 143 F.3d 362 (7th Cir. 1998).

Chapter 5

Mergers: Horizontal, Vertical, and Conglomerate

5D. Horizontal Mergers

Page 861. After **Horizontal Merger Guidelines,** *add the following:*

FEDERAL TRADE COMMISSION v. STAPLES
970 F. Supp. 1066 (D.D.C. 1997)

HOGAN, District Judge. . . . [T]he Federal Trade Commission seeks . . . to enjoin the consummation of any acquisition by defendant Staples of defendant Office Depot pending final disposition before the Commission of administrative proceedings to determine whether such acquisition may substantially lessen competition in violation of Section 7 of the Clayton Act and Section 5 of the Federal Trade Commission Act. The proposed acquisition has been postponed pending the Court's decision on the motion for a preliminary injunction, which is now before the Court for decision after a five-day evidentiary hearing and the filing of proposed findings of fact and conclusions of law. For the reasons set forth below, the Court will grant the plaintiff's motion. . . .

BACKGROUND

... Defendants are both corporations which sell office products—including office supplies, business machines, computers and furniture—through retail stores, commonly described as office supply superstores, as well as through direct mail delivery and contract stationer operations. Staples is the second largest office superstore chain in the United States with approximately 550 retail stores located in 28 states and the District of Columbia, primarily in the Northeast and California. In 1996 Staples' revenues from those stores were approximately $4 billion through all operations. Office Depot, the largest office superstore chain, operates over 500 retail office supply superstores that are located in 38 states and the District of Columbia, primarily in the South and Midwest. Office Depot's 1996 sales were approximately $6.1 billion. OfficeMax is the only other office supply superstore firm in the United States.

On September 4, 1996, defendants Staples and Office Depot . . . entered into an "Agreement and Plan of Merger". . . . Pursuant to the Hart-Scott-Rodino Improvements Act of 1976, Staples and Office Depot filed a Premerger Notification and Report Form with the FTC and Department of Justice on October 2, 1996. This was followed by a seven month investigation by the FTC. The FTC issued a Second Request for Information on November 1, 1996, to both Staples and Office Depot. The Commission further initiated a second Second Request on January 10, 1997. In addition to the hundreds of boxes of documents produced to the FTC during this time, the FTC took depositions of 18 Staples and Office Depot officers and employees. The FTC also undertook extensive ex parte discovery of third-party documents and, in lieu of subpoenas, obtained at least 36 declarations from third parties.

On March 10, 1997, the Commission voted 4-1 to challenge the merger and authorized commencement of an action . . . to seek a temporary restraining order and a preliminary injunction barring the merger. Following this vote, the defendants and the FTC staff negotiated a consent decree that would have authorized the merger to proceed on the condition that Staples and Office Depot sell 63 stores to OfficeMax. However, the Commission voted 3-2 to reject the proposed consent decree on April 4, 1997. The FTC then filed this suit on April 9, 1997, seeking a temporary restraining order and preliminary injunction against the merger. . . .

Because of the urgency of this matter, the Court authorized expedited discovery and held a five-day evidentiary hearing beginning on May 19, 1997. Closing arguments were heard on June 5, 1997. In the meantime, the defendants agreed to postpone the merger pending the Court's decision on the motion for a preliminary injunction, thus making the plaintiff's motion for a temporary restraining order moot. At the hearing, the FTC called a number of live witnesses, including three industry witnesses and two economic experts, Dr. Frederick R. Warren-Boulton and Dr. Orley Ashenfelter. Defendants offered testimony from eight live witnesses, including one economic expert, Dr. Jerry Hausman, as well as an expert in retailing, Maurice Segall. In addition to these live witnesses, the plaintiff and the defendants combined submitted over six thousand exhibits including declarations from consumers, industry analysts, economic experts, suppliers, and other sellers of office supplies. . . .

DISCUSSION

I. Section 13(B) Standard for Preliminary Injunctive Relief

. . . [I]n a suit for preliminary relief, the FTC is not required to prove, nor is the Court required to find, that the proposed merger would in fact violate Section 7 of the Clayton Act. . . . The determination of whether the acquisition actually violates the antitrust laws is reserved for the Commission and is, therefore, not before this Court. . . . Section 13(b) of the Federal Trade Commission Act provides that "[u]pon a proper showing that, weighing the equities and considering the Commission's likelihood of ultimate success, such action would be in the public interest, and after notice to the defendant, a temporary restraining order or a preliminary injunction may be granted without bond."[2] . . .

It is not enough for the FTC to show merely that it has a "fair and tenable chance" of ultimate success on the merits as has been argued and rejected in other cases. . . . However, the FTC need not prove to a certainty that the merger will have an anti-competitive effect. That is a question left to the Commission after a full administrative hearing. Instead, in a suit for a preliminary injunction, the government need only show that there is a "reasonable probability" that the challenged transaction will substantially impair competition. . . .

---

[2] The traditional "irreparable harm" element is absent from the Section 13(b) standard. In this respect, the section 13(b) standard is "lesser" than that which courts normally impose on private litigants seeking a preliminary injunction.

II. The Geographic Market

One of the few issues about which the parties to this case do not disagree is that metropolitan areas are the appropriate geographic markets for analyzing the competitive effects of the proposed merger. . . .

III. The Relevant Product Market

In contrast to the parties' agreement with respect to the relevant geographic market, the Commission and the defendants sharply disagree with respect to the appropriate definition of the relevant product market or line of commerce. As with many antitrust cases, the definition of the relevant product market in this case is crucial. In fact, to a great extent, this case hinges on the proper definition of the relevant product market.

The Commission defines the relevant product market as "the sale of consumable office supplies through office superstores,"[7] with "consumable" meaning products that consumers buy recurrently, i.e., items which "get used up" or discarded. For example, under the Commission's definition, "consumable office supplies" would not include capital goods such as computers, fax machines, and other business machines or office furniture, but does include such products as paper, pens, file folders, post-it notes, computer disks, and toner cartridges. The defendants characterize the FTC's product market definition as "contrived" with no basis in law or fact, and counter that the appropriate product market within which to assess the likely competitive consequences of a Staples-Office Depot combination is simply the overall sale of office products, of which a combined Staples-Office Depot accounted for 5.5% of total sales in North America in 1996. In addition, the defendants argue that the challenged combination is not likely "substantially to lessen competition" however the product market is defined. After considering the arguments on both sides and all of the evidence in this case and making evaluations of each witness's credibility as well as the weight that the Court should give certain evidence and testimony, the Court finds that the appropriate relevant product market definition in this case is, as the Commission has argued, the sale of consumable office supplies through office supply superstores.

---

[7] The Commission also offered an alternative product market, that of the sale of consumable office supplies through retail stores to small businesses and individuals with home offices.

The general rule when determining a relevant product market is that "[t]he outer boundaries of a product market are determined by the reasonable interchangeability of use [by consumers] or the cross-elasticity of demand between the product itself and substitutes for it." *Brown Shoe;* see also *Cellophane*. Interchangeability of use and cross-elasticity of demand look to the availability of substitute commodities, i.e. whether there are other products offered to consumers which are similar in character or use to the product or products in question, as well as how far buyers will go to substitute one commodity for another. *Cellophane*. In other words, the general question is "whether two products can be used for the same purpose, and if so, whether and to what extent purchasers are willing to substitute one for the other." Hayden Pub. Co. v. Cox Broadcasting Corp., 730 F.2d 64, 70 n.8 (2d Cir. 1984).

Whether there are other products available to consumers which are similar in character or use to the products in question may be termed "functional interchangeability.". . . This case, of course, is an example of perfect "functional interchangeability." The consumable office products at issue here are identical whether they are sold by Staples or Office Depot or another seller of office supplies. A legal pad sold by Staples or Office Depot is "functionally interchangeable" with a legal pad sold by Wal-Mart. A post-it note sold by Staples or Office Depot is "functionally interchangeable" with a post-it note sold by Viking or Quill. A computer disk sold by Staples-Office Depot is "functionally interchangeable" with a computer disk sold by CompUSA. No one disputes the functional interchangeability of consumable office supplies. However, as the government has argued, functional interchangeability should not end the Court's analysis.

The Supreme Court did not stop after finding a high degree of functional interchangeability between cellophane and other wrapping materials in the *Cellophane* case. Instead, the Court also found that "an element for consideration as to cross-elasticity of demand between products is the responsiveness of the sales of one product to price changes of the other." For example, in that case, the Court explained, "[i]f a slight decrease in the price of cellophane causes a considerable number of customers of other flexible wrappings to switch to cellophane, it would be an indication that a high cross-elasticity of demand exists between [cellophane and other flexible wrappings], [and therefore] that the products compete in the same market." Following that reasoning in this case, the Commission has argued that a slight but significant increase in Staples-Office Depot's prices will not cause a considerable number of Staples-Office Depot's customers to purchase consumable office supplies from other non-superstore alternatives such as Wal-Mart, Best Buy, Quill, or Viking. On the other hand, the Commission has argued that an increase in price by Staples would result in consumers turning to another office superstore, especially Office Depot, if the consumers had that option. Therefore, the Commission concludes that the sale of consumable office supplies by office supply superstores is the appropriate relevant product market in this case, and products sold by competitors such as Wal-Mart, Best Buy, Viking, Quill, and others should be excluded.

The Court recognizes that it is difficult to overcome the first blush or initial gut reaction of many people to the definition of the relevant product market as the sale of consumable office supplies through office supply superstores. The products in question are undeniably the same no matter who sells them, and no one denies that many different types of retailers sell these products. After all, a combined Staples-Office Depot would only have a 5.5% share of the overall market in consumable office supplies. Therefore, it is logical to conclude that, of course, all these retailers compete, and that if a combined Staples-Office Depot raised prices after the merger, or at least did not lower them as much as they would have as separate companies, that consumers, with such a plethora of options, would shop elsewhere.

The Court acknowledges that there is, in fact, a broad market encompassing the sale of consumable office supplies by all sellers of such supplies, and that those sellers must, at some level, compete with one another. However, the mere fact that a firm may be termed a competitor in the overall marketplace does not necessarily require that it be included in the relevant product market for antitrust purposes. The Supreme Court has recognized that within a broad market, "well-defined submarkets may exist which, in themselves, constitute product markets for antitrust purposes." *Brown Shoe*. . . . With respect to such submarkets, the Court explained "[b]ecause Section 7 of the Clayton Act prohibits any merger which may substantially lessen competition 'in any line of commerce', it is necessary to examine the effects of a merger in each such economically significant submarket to determine if there is a reasonable probability that the merger will substantially lessen competition. If such a probability is found to exist, the merger is proscribed." There is a possibility, therefore, that the sale of consumable office supplies by office superstores may qualify as a submarket within a larger market of retailers of office supplies in general.

The Court in *Brown Shoe* provided a series of factors or "practical indicia" for determining whether a submarket exists including "industry or public recognition of the submarket as a separate economic entity, the product's peculiar characteristics and uses, unique production facilities, distinct customers, distinct prices, sensitivity to price changes, and specialized vendors."

Staples ¶527

Since the Court described these factors as "practical indicia" rather than requirements, subsequent cases have found that submarkets can exist even if only some of these factors are present. . . .

The Commission discussed several of the *Brown Shoe* "practical indicia" in its case, such as industry recognition, and the special characteristics of superstores which make them different from other sellers of office supplies, including distinct formats, customers, and prices. Primarily, however, the FTC focused on what it termed the "pricing evidence," which the Court finds corresponds with *Brown Shoe's* "sensitivity to price changes" factor. First, the FTC presented evidence comparing Staples' prices in geographic markets where Staples is the only office superstore, to markets where Staples competes with Office Depot or OfficeMax, or both. Based on the FTC's calculations, in markets where Staples faces no office superstore competition at all, something which was termed a one firm market during the hearing, prices are 13% higher than in three firm markets where it competes with both Office Depot and OfficeMax. The data which underlie this conclusion make it compelling evidence. Prices were compared as of January 1997, which, admittedly, only provides data for one specific point in time. However, rather than comparing prices from only a small sampling or "basket" of goods, the FTC used an office supply sample accounting for 90% of Staples' sales and comprised of both price sensitive and non-price sensitive items. The FTC presented similar evidence based on Office Depot's prices of a sample of 500 items, also as of January 1997. Similarly, the evidence showed that Office Depot's prices are significantly higher—well over 5% higher,[8] in Depot-only markets than they are in three firm markets.

Other pricing evidence presented by the FTC is less convincing on its own, due to limitations in the underlying data. For example, relatively small samplings or "baskets" of goods may have been used or it may not be clear how many stock keeping units ("SKUs") of supplies were included. For example, the FTC also presented evidence comparing Staples' prices in Staples-only markets with Staples' prices in three-firm markets for four different time periods, August 1994, January 1995, August 1995, and May 1996. The result is startlingly similar to that found in the first two examples. Where Staples

---

[8] The analytical framework set forth in the Merger Guidelines approaches the inquiry regarding the reasonable interchangeability of use or cross-elasticity of demand by asking whether a "hypothetical monopolist would profitably impose at least a 'small but significant and nontransitory' [price] increase." Merger Guidelines at §1.11. The Merger Guidelines use 5% of the usual approximation of a "small but significant and nontransitory increase." For this reason, the Court's analysis will often refer to this 5% number.

does not compete with other office superstores, it charges prices well over 5% higher than where it does so compete. While having the advantage of showing a trend over time, the Court recognizes that this evidence has some problems. These particular calculations were made based on a "basket" or sample of supplies comprised of supplies used by Staples to price check against Office Depot. The number of SKUs in the sample was not provided to the Court, and it appears that the components of the baskets may have changed over time. Therefore, the Court would not give much weight to this evidence standing alone. However, since additional evidence supports the same conclusion, the Court credits this evidence as confirmation of the general pricing trend.

The FTC also pointed to internal Staples documents which present price comparisons between Staples' prices and Office Depot's prices and Staples' prices and OfficeMax's prices within different price zones.[9] The comparisons between Staples and Office Depot were made in August 1994, January 1995, August 1995, and May 1996. Staples' prices were compared with Office-Max's prices in August 1994, July 1995, and January 1996. For each comparison, Staples' calculations were based on a fairly large "basket" or sample of goods, approximately 2000 SKUs containing both price sensitive and non-price sensitive items. Using Staples' data, but organizing it differently to show which of those zones were one, two, or three firm markets, the FTC showed once again that Staples charges significantly higher prices, more than 5% higher, where it has no office superstore competition than where it competes with the two other superstores.

The FTC offered similar price comparison evidence for Office Depot, comparing Office Depot's prices across Staples' zones. The comparisons were made in August 1994, January 1995, August 1995, and May 1996. Again, a large sample, approximately 2000 SKUs, was considered. The results of this analysis are slightly less favorable to the FTC's position. Price differentials are significantly smaller and there are even a few instances where Office Depot's prices appear to be higher in one of its three firm markets than prices in its two firm markets and at least one point where prices in one of the Depot-only zones were lower than prices in one of the three firm markets. On average, however, this evidence shows that Office Depot's prices are highest in its one firm markets, and lowest in its three firm markets.

---

[9] It was established at the hearing that Staples and Office Depot do not maintain nationally uniform prices in their stores. Instead, both companies currently organize their stores into price zones which are simply groups of one or more stores that have common prices.

Staples ¶527

This evidence all suggests that office superstore prices are affected primarily by other office superstores and not by non-superstore competitors such as mass merchandisers like Wal-Mart, Kmart, or Target, wholesale clubs such as BJ's, Sam's, and Price Costco, computer or electronic stores such as Computer City and Best Buy, independent retail office supply stores, mail order firms like Quill and Viking, and contract stationers. Though the FTC did not present the Court with evidence regarding the precise amount of non-superstore competition in each of Staples' and Office Depot's one, two, and three firm markets, it is clear to the Court that these competitors, albeit in different combinations and concentrations, are present in every one of these markets. For example, it is a certainty that the mail order competitors compete in all of the geographic markets at issue in this case. Office products are available through the mail in all 50 states, and have been for approximately 30 years. Despite this mail order competition, however, Staples and Office Depot are still able to charge higher prices in their one firm markets than they do in the two firm markets and the three firm markets without losing a significant number of customers to the mail order firms. The same appears to be true with respect to Wal-Mart. Bill Long, Vice President for Merchandising at Wal-Mart Stores, testifying through declaration, explained that price-checking by Wal-Mart of Staples' prices in areas where both Staples and Wal-Mart exist showed that, on average, Staples' prices were higher where there was a Staples and a Wal-Mart but no other superstore than where there was a Staples, a Wal-Mart, and another superstore.

The evidence with respect to the wholesale club stores is consistent. Mike Atkinson, Vice President, Division Merchandise Manager of BJ's Wholesale Club, testified at the hearing regarding BJ's price checking of Staples and Office Depot in areas where BJ's competes with one or both of those superstores. Though his sample was small—he testified that less than 10% of BJ's 80 stores are located in the same area as a Staples and/or Office Depot—BJ's price checking found that, in general, office supply superstore prices were lowest where there was both a Staples and an Office Depot. In addition, Staples' own pricing information shows that warehouse clubs have very little effect on Staples' prices. For example, Staples' maintains a "warehouse club only" price zone, which indicates a zone where Staples exists with a warehouse club but without another office superstore. The data presented by the Commission on Staples' pricing shows only a slight variation in prices (1%-2%) between "warehouse club only" zones and one superstore markets without a warehouse club. Additionally, in May 1996, two price comparison studies done by Staples, first using 2,084 SKUs including both price sensitive

93

¶527

and non-price sensitive items and then using only 244 SKUs of price sensitive items, showed that prices in the "club only" zones, on average, were over 10% higher than in zones where Staples competes with Office Depot and/or OfficeMax.

There is also consistent evidence with respect to computer and/or consumer electronics stores such as Best Buy. For example, Office Depot maintains a separate price zone, which it calls "zone 30," for areas with Best Buy locations but no other office supply superstores. However, the FTC introduced evidence, based on a January 1997 market basket of "top 500 items by velocity," that prices in Office Depot's "zone 30" price zone are almost as high as in its "non-competitive" price zone, the zone where it does not compete with another office superstore.

There is similar evidence with respect to the defendants' behavior when faced with entry of another competitor. The evidence shows that the defendants change their price zones when faced with entry of another superstore, but do not do so for other retailers. For example, Staples changed its price zone for Cincinnati to a lower priced zone when Office Depot and OfficeMax entered that area. New entry by Staples and OfficeMax caused a decline in prices at Office Depot's Greensboro stores. In July 1996, after OfficeMax entered Jackson, Michigan, Staples moved its Jackson store to a new zone, cutting prices by 6%. There are numerous additional examples of zones being changed and prices falling as a result of superstore entry. There is no evidence that zones change and prices fall when another non-superstore retailer enters a geographic market.

Though individually the FTC's evidence can be criticized for looking at only brief snapshots in time or for considering only a limited number of SKUs, taken together, however, the Court finds this evidence a compelling showing that a small but significant increase in Staples' prices will not cause a significant number of consumers to turn to non-superstore alternatives for purchasing their consumable office supplies. Despite the high degree of functional interchangeability between consumable office supplies sold by the office superstores and other retailers of office supplies, the evidence presented by the Commission shows that even where Staples and Office Depot charge higher prices, certain consumers do not go elsewhere for their supplies. This further demonstrates that the sale of office supplies by non- superstore retailers is not responsive to the higher prices charged by Staples and Office Depot in the one firm markets. This indicates a low cross-elasticity of demand between the consumable office supplies sold by the superstores and those sold by other sellers.

Turning back to the other *Brown Shoe* "practical indicia" of submarkets that the Commission offered in this case, the Commission presented and the Court heard a great deal of testimony at the hearing and through declarations about the uniqueness of office superstores and the differences between the office superstores and other sellers of office supplies such as mass merchandisers, wholesale clubs, and mail order firms as well as the special characteristics of office superstore customers. In addition, the Court was asked to go and view many of the different types of retail formats. That evidence shows that office superstores are, in fact, very different in appearance, physical size, format, the number and variety of SKUs offered, and the type of customers targeted and served than other sellers of office supplies.

The Court has observed that office supply superstores look far different from other sellers of office supplies. Office supply superstores are high volume, discount office supply chain stores averaging in excess of 20,000 square feet, with over 11,000 of those square feet devoted to traditional office supplies, and carrying over 5,000 SKUs of consumable office supplies in addition to computers, office furniture, and other non-consumables. In contrast, stores such as Kmart devote approximately 210 square feet to the sale of approximately 250 SKUs of consumable office supplies. Kinko's devotes approximately 50 square feet to the sale of 150 SKUs. Target sells only 400 SKUs. Both Sam's Club and Computer City each sell approximately 200 SKUs. Even if these SKU totals are low estimates as the defendants have argued, there is still a huge difference between the superstores and the rest of the office supply sellers.

In addition to the differences in SKU numbers and variety, the superstores are different from many other sellers of office supplies due to the type of customer they target and attract. The superstores' customer base overwhelmingly consists of small businesses with fewer than 20 employees and consumers with home offices. In contrast, mail order customers are typically mid-sized companies with more than 20 employees. Another example is contract stationers who focus on serving customers with more than 100 employees. While the Court accepts that some small businesses with fewer than 20 employees as well as home office customers do choose other sellers of office supplies, the superstores' customers are different from those of many of the purported competitors.

It is difficult to fully articulate and explain all of the ways in which superstores are unique. As the plaintiff and defendant requested, the Court viewed some of the various sellers of office supplies located in the Rockville, Maryland area, including Staples, Office Depot, CompUSA, Best Buy, CVS,

Kmart, Giant Food, and Wal-Mart. Based on the Court's observations, the Court finds that the unique combination of size, selection, depth and breadth of inventory offered by the superstores distinguishes them from other retailers. Other retailers devote only a fraction of their square footage to office supplies as opposed to Staples or Office Depot. The evidence shows that the typical club, mass merchant, or computer store offers only 210 to 2000 square feet of office supplies, compared to over 11,182 square feet at a typical Staples. This was evident to the Court when visiting the various stores. Superstores are simply different in scale and appearance from the other retailers. No one entering a Wal-Mart would mistake it for an office superstore. No one entering Staples or Office Depot would mistakenly think he or she was in Best Buy or CompUSA. You certainly know an office superstore when you see one. . . .

Another of the "practical indicia" for determining the presence of a submarket suggested by *Brown Shoe* is "industry or public recognition of the submarket as a separate economic entity." See also Rothery Storage & Van Co. v. Atlas Van Lines, 792 F.2d 210, 219 (D.C. Cir. 1986) (Bork, J.) ("The industry or public recognition of the submarket as a separate economic unit matters because we assume that economic actors usually have accurate perceptions of economic realities."), cert. denied, 479 U.S. 1033 (1987); FTC v. Coca-Cola Co., 641 F. Supp. 1128, 1132 (D.D.C. 1986) ("Analysis of the market is a matter of business reality—a matter of how the market is perceived by those who strive for profit in it"), vacated as moot, 829 F.2d 191 (D.C. Cir. 1987). The Commission offered abundant evidence on this factor from Staples' and Office Depot's documents which shows that both Staples and Office Depot focus primarily on competition from other superstores. The documents reviewed by the Court show that the merging parties evaluate their "competition" as the other office superstore firms, without reference to other retailers, mail order firms, or independent stationers. In document after document, the parties refer to, discuss, and make business decisions based upon the assumption that "competition" refers to other office superstores only. For example, Staples uses the phrase "office superstore industry" in strategic planning documents. Staples' 1996 Strategy Update refers to the "Big Three" and "improved relative competitive position" since 1993 and states that Staples is "increasingly recognized as [the] industry leader." A document analyzing a possible acquisition of OfficeMax referenced the "benefits from pricing in [newly] noncompetitive markets," and also the fact that there was "a potential margin lift overall as the industry moves to 2 players."

Staples ¶527

When assessing key trends and making long range plans, Staples and Office Depot focus on the plans of other superstores. In addition, when determining whether to enter a new metropolitan area, both Staples and Office Depot evaluate the extent of office superstore competition in the market and the number of office superstores the market can support. When selecting sites and markets for new store openings, defendants repeatedly refer to markets without office superstores as "non-competitive," even when the new store is adjacent to or near a warehouse club, consumer electronics store, or a mass merchandiser such as Wal-Mart. In a monthly report entitled "Competitor Store Opening/Closing Report" which Office Depot circulates to its Executive Committee, Office Depot notes all competitor store closings and openings, but the only competitors referred to for its United States stores are Staples and OfficeMax.

While it is clear to the Court that Staples and Office Depot do not ignore sellers such as warehouse clubs, Best Buy, or Wal-Mart, the evidence clearly shows that Staples and Office Depot each consider the other superstores as the primary competition. For example, Office Depot has a Best Buy zone and Staples has a warehouse club zone. However, each still refers to its one firm markets with no other office superstore as "non-competitive" zones or markets. In addition, it is clear from the evidence that Staples and Office Depot price check the other office superstores much more frequently and extensively than they price check other retailers such as BJ's or Best Buy, and that Staples and Office Depot are more concerned with keeping their prices in parity with the other office superstores in their geographic areas than in undercutting Best Buy or a warehouse club.

For the reasons set forth in the above analysis, the Court finds that the sale of consumable office supplies through office supply superstores is the appropriate relevant product market for purposes of considering the possible anticompetitive effects of the proposed merger between Staples and Office Depot. The pricing evidence indicates a low cross-elasticity of demand between consumable office products sold by Staples or Office Depot and those same products sold by other sellers of office supplies. This same evidence indicates that non-superstore sellers of office supplies are not able to effectively constrain the superstores' prices, because a significant number of superstore customers do not turn to a non-superstore alternative when faced with higher prices in the one firm markets. In addition, the factors or "practical indicia" of *Brown Shoe* support a finding of a "submarket" under the facts of this case, and "submarkets," as *Brown Shoe* established, may themselves be appropriate product markets for antitrust purposes.[11] . . .

IV. Probable Effect on Competition

After accepting the Commission's definition of the relevant product market, the Court next must consider the probable effect of a merger between Staples and Office Depot in the geographic markets previously identified. One way to do this is to examine the concentration statistics and HHIs within the geographic markets. If the relevant product market is defined as the sale of consumable office supplies through office supply superstores, the HHIs in many of the geographic markets are at problematic levels even before the merger. Currently, the least concentrated market is that of Grand Rapids-Muskegon-Holland, Michigan, with an HHI of 3,597, while the most concentrated is Washington, D.C. with an HHI of 6,944. In contrast, after a merger of Staples and Office Depot, the least concentrated area would be Kalamazoo-Battle Creek Michigan, with an HHI of 5,003, and many areas would have HHIs of 10,000. The average increase in HHI caused by the merger would be 2,715 points. The concentration statistics show that a merged Staples-Office Depot would have a dominant market share in 42 geographic markets across the country. The combined shares of Staples and Office Depot in the office superstore market would be 100% in 15 metropolitan areas. It is in these markets that the post-merger HHI would be 10,000. In 27 other metropolitan areas, where the number of office superstore competitors would drop from three to two, the post-merger market shares would range from 45% to 94%, with post-merger HHIs ranging from 5,003 to 9,049. Even the lowest of these HHIs indicates a "highly concentrated" market.

According to the Department of Justice Merger Guidelines, a market with an HHI of less than 1,000 is "unconcentrated." An HHI between 1,000 and 1,800 indicates a "moderately concentrated" market, and any market with an HHI over 1,800 qualifies as "highly concentrated." See FTC v. PPG Indus., 798 F.2d 1500, 1503 (D.C. Cir. 1986) (citing the Merger Guidelines).

---

[11] As other courts have noted, use of the term "submarket" may be confusing. See Allen-Myland v. IBM Corp., 33 F.3d 194, 208 n.16 (3rd Cir.1994) (finding it less confusing to speak in terms of the relevant product market rather than the submarket), cert. denied, 513 U.S. 1066 (1994); Olin Corp. v. FTC, 986 F.2d 1295, 1299 (9th Cir.1993) ("[E]very market that encompasses less than all products is, in a sense, a submarket"), cert. denied, 510 U.S. 1110 (1994). Whatever term is used—market, submarket, relevant product market—the analysis is the same.

Further, according to the Merger Guidelines, unless mitigated by other factors which lead to the conclusion that the merger is not likely to lessen competition, an increase in the HHI is excess of 50 points in a post-merger highly concentrated market may raise significant competitive concerns. In cases where the post-merger HHI is less than 1,800, but greater than 1,000, the Merger Guidelines presume that a 100 point increase in the HHI is evidence that the merger will create or enhance market power. The Merger Guidelines, of course, are not binding on the Court, but, as this Circuit has stated, they do provide "a useful illustration of the application of the HHI," and the Court will use that guidance here. In addition, though the Supreme Court has established that there is no fixed threshold at which an increase in market concentration triggers the antitrust laws, see, e.g., *Philadelphia Bank,* this is clearly not a borderline case. The pre-merger markets are already in the "highly concentrated" range, and the post-merger HHIs show an average increase of 2,715 points. Therefore, the Court finds that the plaintiffs have shown a likelihood of success on the merits. With HHIs of this level, the Commission certainly has shown a "reasonable probability" that the proposed merger would have an anti-competitive effect.[13]

The HHI calculations and market concentration evidence, however, are not the only indications that a merger between Staples and Office Depot may substantially lessen competition. Much of the evidence already discussed with respect to defining the relevant product market also indicates that the merger would likely have an anti-competitive effect. The evidence of the defendants' own current pricing practices, for example, shows that an office superstore chain facing no competition from other superstores has the ability to profitably raise prices for consumable office supplies above competitive levels. The fact that Staples and Office Depot both charge higher prices

---

[13] . . . In response to the defendants' arguments regarding the variety of competition in this larger office supply market, the Commission presented HHI calculations which included additional competitors. Besides Staples, Office Depot, and OfficeMax, the Commission included Price Costco, Sam's Club, BJ's, Best Buy, Wal-Mart, Kmart, Target, Circuit City, Computer City, CompUSA, and independent office supply dealers in this alternate HHI calculation. The result showed Sacramento, California as the least concentrated market post-merger with an HHI of 1,793, and Greenville, North Carolina as the most concentrated market post-merger with an HHI of 5,047. Overall, the HHIs increased by an average of 861 points post-merger, an increase that is still problematic according to the Merger Guidelines given that all the post-merger markets were in the "moderately" or "highly concentrated" range. Therefore, for this reason as well, the Court finds that the Commission has shown a "reasonable probability" that the merger would have an anti-competitive effect.

¶527

where they face no superstore competition demonstrates that an office superstore can raise prices above competitive levels. The evidence also shows that defendants also change their price zones when faced with entry of another office superstore, but do not do so for other retailers. Since prices are significantly lower in markets where Staples and Office Depot compete, eliminating this competition with one another would free the parties to charge higher prices in those markets, especially those in which the combined entity would be the sole office superstore. In addition, allowing the defendants to merge would eliminate significant future competition. Absent the merger, the firms are likely, and in fact have planned, to enter more of each other's markets, leading to a deconcentration of the market and, therefore, increased competition between the superstores.

In addition, direct evidence shows that by eliminating Staples' most significant, and in many markets only, rival, this merger would allow Staples to increase prices or otherwise maintain prices at an anti-competitive level. The merger would eliminate significant head-to-head competition between the two lowest cost and lowest priced firms in the superstore market. Thus, the merger would result in the elimination of a particularly aggressive competitor in a highly concentrated market, a factor which is certainly an important consideration when analyzing possible anti-competitive effects. . . . It is based on all of this evidence as well that the Court finds that the Commission has shown a likelihood of success on the merits and a "reasonable probability" that the proposed transaction will have an anti-competitive effect.

By showing that the proposed transaction between Staples and Office Depot will lead to undue concentration in the market for consumable office supplies sold by office superstores in the geographic markets agreed upon by the parties, the Commission establishes a presumption that the transaction will substantially lessen competition. . . . *Philadelphia Bank.* Once such a presumption has been established, the burden of producing evidence to rebut the presumption shifts to the defendants. . . . *General Dynamics.* To meet this burden, the defendants must show that the market-share statistics give an inaccurate prediction of the proposed acquisition's probable effect on competition. . . . In order to rebut the FTC's showing with respect to the likely anti-competitive effects of a merger, defendants challenged the FTC's market-share statistics in this case in various ways, such as criticizing the Commission's definition of the relevant product market and introducing evidence to counter the FTC's pricing information. Defendants' also made allegations of "cherry-picking" on the part of the Commission, pointing to data which tend to show the opposite from the Commission's contentions. Finally, the defendants argued that the price differentials between one, two, and three firm markets shown by the Commission do not accurately reflect market power because the Commission failed to take into account factors such as the differences in marketing costs between stores.

In their criticism of the Commission's pricing evidence, the defendants accused the FTC of "cherry-picking" its data and pointed to specific examples which contradict the Commission's conclusions. For example, the defendants focused on the FTC's comparison prices on manila folders in two Ohio towns, Columbus which has two superstores and Cincinnati which has all three superstore chains. For 1995-96, the prices of those manila folders were shown to be, on average, 51% higher in the two firm market than in the three firm market. The defendants argued that in contrast to the Ohio example, a comparison of two Indiana towns, Kokomo with two firms and Elkhart/South Bend with all three firms, shows the opposite. In fact, the defendants' comparison of the average prices of manila folders for 1996 in Kokomo and Elkhart/South Bend shows that the prices in Kokomo, the two firm market, were 30% lower than in the three firm market.

The Court acknowledges that there is some evidence of this type in the record, and the Court has considered all of it. However, the fact that there may be some examples with respect to individual items in individual cities which contradict the FTC's evidence does not overly concern the Court. A few examples of isolated products simply cannot refute the power of the FTC's evidence with respect to the overall trend over time, which is that Staples' and Office Depot's prices are lowest in three firm markets and highest where they do not compete with another office superstore. Neither does the fact that some two superstore areas have lower prices than some three firm markets. In addition, a closer examination of the price comparison study done by the defendants for Kokomo and Elkhart/South Bend shows that for four of the six products compared, the prices were actually higher in Kokomo. Moreover, when Staples' total of price sensitive and non-price sensitive items are examined, Kokomo's prices are between 3 and 5% higher than Elkhart, which reconfirms the Commission's result rather than refuting it.

Defendants also argued that the regional price differences set forth in the FTC's pricing evidence do not reflect market power, because the reason for those differentials is not solely the presence or absence of other superstore competition. Instead, argued the defendants, these differentials are the result of a host of factors other than superstore competition. As examples of other factors which cause differences in pricing between geographic markets, the defendants offered sales volume, product mix, marketing or advertising costs, and distribution costs. Defendants also argued that there are differences in wages and rent which cause the differences in pricing between certain stores. The Court, however, cannot find that the evidence submitted by the defendants with respect to other reasons for the differences in pricing between one, two, and three firm markets is sufficient to rebut the Commission's evidence.

The Court generally accepts that per-store advertising costs, such as those incurred for a newspaper insert, will likely be lower in markets where Staples or Office Depot has a larger number of stores as those costs may be spread over a larger number of stores, and the defendants have provided some concrete evidence that the price differentials shown by the FTC may be somewhat affected by marketing costs. . . . These numbers do suggest a correlation between the prices charged by Staples and marketing costs as average marketing costs are higher in the one firm markets than the three firm markets. However, the marketing cost evidence also shows that marketing costs are lower in Staples/Depot areas than in Staples/OfficeMax areas and, in fact, that costs are higher in Staples/OfficeMax areas than in the three firm markets, which does not correspond with the pricing trend. Staples generally charges lower prices where it competes with Office Depot than where it competes with OfficeMax and generally charges lower prices in three firm markets than in Staples/OfficeMax areas. In addition, the differences in marketing costs are not so large that they alone could account for the significant price differentials shown by the FTC.

As the Court has already noted, the defendants, of course, point to other factors besides marketing costs. However, unlike the comparison of average marketing costs between one, two, and three firm markets, the defendants produced no concrete evidence in support of these other factors. For example, the Court believes that it is probably true that distribution costs are higher for stores which are the farthest from either company's distribution centers. Yet, the defendants introduced no evidence to show that the one firm markets are, in fact, the farthest from distribution centers or that in the three firm markets, the stores are the closest to the distribution centers. Nor did the defendants introduce any evidence showing the actual differences in distribution costs based on a store's distance from a distribution center. The only evidence that the Court heard on this point was the testimony of Thomas Stemberg, Chairman and CEO of Staples, who testified at the hearing that "typically the smaller markets are further away from the distribution hubs. It costs you a lot more to haul freight up to Bangor, Maine, than it does from Hagerstown to Washington." The Court cannot find that the FTC's pricing evidence is seriously undermined by such a general statement.

Staples ¶527

The defendants' evidence is similar with respect to sales volume, rent and wages. For example, Steven Mandel, Senior Managing Director of Tiger Management Corporation, testified at the hearing that single store markets are typically smaller markets. He continued by explaining that even though the costs of rent and labor may be lower in a smaller market, they would be higher as a percentage of sales because the volume of sales is also typically lower in these smaller markets. Therefore, in order to come out with a decent return on investment, it will be necessary to have a modestly higher gross margin in those markets. While this seems logical to the Court, again, the only evidence presented on the point is very general and the Court cannot give it much weight. . . .

V. Entry Into the Market

"The existence and significance of barriers to entry are frequently, of course, crucial considerations in a rebuttal analysis [because] [i]n the absence of significant barriers, a company probably cannot maintain supra-competitive pricing for any length of time." United States v. Baker Hughes, 908 F.2d 981, 987 (D.C. Cir. 1990). Thus, the Court must consider whether, in this case, "entry into the market would likely avert anticompetitive effects from [Staples'] acquisition of [Office Depot]." Id. at 989. If the defendants' evidence regarding entry showed that the Commission's market-share statistics give an incorrect prediction of the proposed acquisition's probable effect on competition because entry into the market would likely avert any anti-competitive effect by acting as a constraint on Staples-Office Depot's prices, the Court would deny the FTC's motion. The Court, however, cannot make such a finding in this case.

The defendants argued during the hearing and in their briefs that the rapid growth in overall office supply sales has encouraged and will continue to encourage expansion and entry. One reason for this, according to Dr. Hausman's declaration, is that entry is more attractive when an industry is growing, because new entrants can establish themselves without having to take all of their sales away from existing competitors. In addition, the defendants' impressive retailing expert, Professor Maurice Segall, testified at the hearing that there are "no barriers to entry in retailing," and defendants pointed to the fact that all office superstore entrants have entered within the last 11 years.

In addition to this general testimony regarding entry, defendants emphasized specific examples of recent or planned entry. . . . There are problems with the defendants' evidence, however, that prevent the Court from finding in this case that entry into the market by new competitors or expansion into

¶527

the market by existing firms would likely avert the anti-competitive effects from Staples' acquisition of Office Depot. For example, while it is true that all office superstore entrants have entered within the last 11 years, the recent trend for office superstores has actually been toward exiting the market rather than entering. Over the past few years, the number of office superstore chains has dramatically dropped from twenty-three to three. All but Staples, Office Depot, and OfficeMax have either closed or been acquired. The failed office superstore entrants include very large, well-known retail establishments such as Kmart, Montgomery Ward, Ames, and Zayres. A new office superstore would need to open a large number of stores nationally in order to achieve the purchasing and distribution economies of scale enjoyed by the three existing firms. Sunk costs would be extremely high. Economies of scale at the local level, such as in the costs of advertising and distribution, would also be difficult for a new superstore entrant to achieve since the three existing firms have saturated many important local markets. . . .

For the reasons discussed above, the Court finds it extremely unlikely that a new office superstore will enter the market and thereby avert the anti-competitive effects from Staples' acquisition of Office Depot. The defendants, of course, focused their entry argument on more than just the entry of additional superstores, pointing also to the expansion of existing companies such as U.S. Office Products and Wal-Mart. The Court also finds it unlikely that the expansions by U.S. Office Products and Wal-Mart would avert the anti-competitive effects which would result from the merger. . . .

The defendants' final argument with respect to entry was that existing retailers such as Sam's Club, Kmart, and Best Buy have the capability to reallocate their shelf space to include additional SKUs of office supplies. While stores such as these certainly do have the power to reallocate shelf space, there is no evidence that they will in fact do this if a combined Staples-Office Depot were to raise prices by 5% following a merger. In fact, the evidence indicates that it is more likely that they would not. For example, even in the superstores' anti-competitive zones where either Staples or Office Depot does not compete with other superstores, no retailer has successfully expanded its consumable office supplies to the extent that it constrains superstore pricing. Best Buy attempted such an expansion by creating an office supplies department in 1994, offering 2000 SKUs of office supplies, but found the expansion less profitable than hoped for and gave up after two years. For these reasons, the Court also cannot find that the ability of many sellers of office supplies to reconfigure shelf space and add SKUs of office supplies is likely to avert anti-competitive effects from Staples' acquisition of Office Depot. The Court will next consider the defendants' efficiencies defense.

Staples ¶527

VI. Efficiencies

Whether an efficiencies defense showing that the intended merger would create significant efficiencies in the relevant market, thereby offsetting any anti-competitive effects, may be used by a defendant to rebut the government's prima facie case is not entirely clear. The newly revised efficiencies section of the Merger Guidelines recognizes that, "mergers have the potential to generate significant efficiencies by permitting a better utilization of existing assets, enabling the combined firm to achieve lower costs in producing a given quality and quantity than either firm could have achieved without the proposed transaction." See Merger Guidelines §4. This coincides with the view of some courts that "whether an acquisition would yield significant efficiencies in the relevant market is an important consideration in predicting whether the acquisition would substantially lessen competition. . . . [T]herefore, . . . an efficiency defense to the government's prima facie case in section 7 challenges is appropriate in certain circumstances." FTC v. University Health, 938 F.2d 1206, 1222 (11th Cir. 1991). The Supreme Court, however, in *Clorox*, stated that "[p]ossible economics cannot be used as a defense to illegality in section 7 merger cases." There has been great disagreement regarding the meaning of this precedent and whether an efficiencies defense is permitted. . . . Neither the Commission [nor] the defendants could point to a case in which this Circuit has spoken on the issue. . . . Assuming that it is a viable defense, however, the Court cannot find in this case that the defendants' efficiencies evidence rebuts the presumption that the merger may substantially lessen competition or shows that the Commission's evidence gives an inaccurate prediction of the proposed acquisition's probable effect.

The Court agrees with the defendants that where, as here, the merger has not yet been consummated, it is impossible to quantify precisely the efficiencies that it will generate. In addition, the Court recognizes a difference between efficiencies which are merely speculative and those which are based on a prediction backed by sound business judgment. Nor does the Court believe that the defendants must prove their efficiencies by "clear and convincing evidence" in order for those efficiencies to be considered by the Court. That would saddle Section 7 defendants with the nearly impossible task of rebutting a possibility with a certainty, a burden which was rejected in *Baker Hughes*, 908 F.2d at 992. Instead, like all rebuttal evidence in Section 7 cases, the defendants must simply rebut the presumption that the merger will substantially lessen competition by showing that the Commission's evidence gives an inaccurate prediction of the proposed acquisition's probable effect.

See id. at 991. Defendants, however, must do this with credible evidence, and the Court with respect to this issue did not find the defendants' evidence to be credible.

Defendants' submitted an "Efficiencies Analysis" which predicated that the combined company would achieve savings of between $4.9 and $6.5 billion over the next five years. In addition, the defendants argued that the merger would also generate dynamic efficiencies. For example, defendants argued that as suppliers become more efficient due to their increased sales volume to the combined Staples-Office Depot, they would be able to lower prices to their other retailers. Moreover, defendants argued that two-thirds of the savings realized by the combined company would be passed along to consumers.

Evaluating credibility, as the Court must do, the Court credits the testimony and Report of the Commission's expert, David Painter, over the testimony and Efficiencies Study of the defendants' efficiencies witness, Shira Goodman, Senior Vice President of Integration at Staples. Mr. Painter's testimony was compelling, and the Court finds, based primarily on Mr. Painter's testimony, that the defendants' cost savings estimates are unreliable. First, the Court notes that the cost savings estimate of $4.947 billion over five years which was submitted to the Court exceeds by almost 500% the figures presented to the two Boards of Directors in September 1996, when the Boards approved the transaction. The cost savings claims submitted to the Court are also substantially greater than those represented in the defendants' Joint Proxy Statement/Prospectus "reflecting the best currently available estimate of management," and filed with the Securities and Exchange Commission on January 23, 1997, or referenced in the "fairness opinions" rendered by the defendants' investment bankers which are contained in the Proxy Statement.

The Court also finds that the defendants' projected "Base Case" savings of $5 billion are in large part unverified, or at least the defendants failed to produce the necessary documentation for verification. One example of this is the estimated cost savings from the Goods and Services category which projects cost savings of $553 million, about 10% of the total cost savings attributed to the merger by the defendants. Ms. Goodman admitted that the entire backup, source, and the calculations of the Goods and Services' cost savings were not included in the Efficiencies Analysis. In addition, Ms. Goodman was unable to explain the methods used to calculate many of the cost savings. Similarly, the projected distribution cost savings, $883 million or 17% of the projected total cost savings, are problematic. Defendants' consultant A.T. Kearney estimated the savings, and Ms. Goodman admitted the Efficiency Analysis did not show that Kearney had deducted the projected Staples stand-alone savings from the new Hagerstown and Los Angeles full line distribution centers.

As with the failure to deduct the Staples stand-alone savings from the new Hagerstown and Los Angeles full line distribution centers from the projected distribution cost savings, the evidence shows that the defendants did not accurately calculate which projected cost savings were merger specific and which were, in fact, not related to the merger. For example, defendants' largest cost savings, over $2 billion or 40% of the total estimate, are projected as a result of their expectation of obtaining better prices from vendors. However, this figure was determined in relation to the cost savings enjoyed by Staples at the end of 1996 without considering the additional cost savings that Staples would have received in the future as a stand-alone company. Since Staples has continuously sought and achieved cost savings on its own, clearly the comparison that should have been made was between the projected future cost savings of Staples as a stand-alone company, not its past rate of savings, and the projected future cost savings of the combined company. Thus, the calculation in the Efficiencies Analysis included product cost savings that Staples and Office Depot would likely have realized without the merger. In fact, Mr. Painter testified that, by his calculation, 43% of the estimated savings are savings that Staples and Office Depot would likely have achieved as stand-alone entities.

There are additional examples of projected savings, such as the projected savings on employee health insurance, which are not merger specific, but the Court need not discuss every example here. However, in addition to the non-merger specific projected savings, Mr. Painter also revealed problems with the defendants' methodology in making some of the projections. For example, in calculating the projected cost savings from vendors, Staples estimated cost savings for a selected group of vendors, and then extrapolated these estimated savings to all other vendors. Mr. Painter testified that, although Hewlett Packard is Staples' single largest vendor, it was not one of the vendors used for the savings estimate. In addition, the evidence shows that Staples was not confident that it could improve its buying from Hewlett Packard. Yet, Staples' purchases and sales of Hewlett Packard products were included in the "all other" vendor group, and defendants, thereby, attributed cost savings in the amount of $207 million to Hewlett Packard even though Staples' personnel did not believe that they could, in fact, achieve cost savings from Hewlett Packard.

In addition to the problems that the Court has with the efficiencies estimates themselves, the Court also finds that the defendants' projected pass through rate—the amount of the projected savings that the combined company expects to pass on to customers in the form of lower prices—is unrealistic. The Court has no doubt that a portion of any efficiencies achieved through a merger of the defendants would be passed on to customers. Staples and Office Depot have a proven track record of achieving cost savings through efficiencies, and then passing those savings to customers in the form of lower prices. However, in this case the defendants have projected a pass through rate of two-thirds of the savings while the evidence shows that, historically, Staples has passed through only 15-17%. Based on the above evidence, the Court cannot find that the defendants have rebutted the presumption that the merger will substantially lessen competition by showing that, because of the efficiencies which will result from the merger, the Commission's evidence gives an inaccurate prediction of the proposed acquisition's probable effect. Therefore, the only remaining issue for the Court is the balancing of the equities.

VII. The Equities

Where, as in this case, the Court finds that the Commission has established a likelihood of success on the merits, a presumption in favor of a preliminary injunction arises. . . . Despite such a presumption, however, once the Court has determined the FTC's likelihood of success on the merits, it must still turn to and consider the equities. . . .

The strong public interest in effective enforcement of the antitrust laws weighs heavily in favor of an injunction in this case, as does the need to preserve meaningful relief following a full administrative trial on the merits. "Unscrambling the eggs" after the fact is not a realistic option in this case. Both the plaintiff as well as the defendants introduced evidence regarding the combined company's post-merger plans, including the consolidation of warehouse and supply facilities in order to integrate the two distribution systems, the closing of 40 to 70 Office Depot and Staples stores, changing the name of the Office Depot stores, negotiating new contracts with manufacturers and suppliers, and, lastly, the consolidation of management which is likely to lead to the loss of employment for many of Office Depot's key personnel. As a result, the Court finds that it is extremely unlikely, if the Court denied the plaintiff's motion and the merger were to go through, that the merger could be effectively undone and the companies divided if the agency later found that the merger violated the antitrust laws. It would not simply be a

Staples ¶527

matter of putting the old Office Depot signs back on the stores. Office Depot would have lost its name, many of its stores, its distribution centers, and key personnel. It would also be behind in future plans to open new stores and expand on its own.

More importantly, in addition to the practical difficulties in undoing the merger, consumers would be at risk of serious anti-competitive harm in the interim. Without an injunction, consumers in the 42 geographic markets where superstore competition would be eliminated or significantly reduced face the prospect of higher prices than they would have absent the merger. These higher charges could never be recouped even if the administrative proceeding resulted in a finding that the merger violated the antitrust laws. Failure to grant a preliminary injunction also would deny consumers the benefit of any new competition that would have occurred, absent the merger, between Staples and Office Depot as those stores continued to enter and compete in each other's markets. Both parties had aggressive expansion plans before the merger, many of which have been put on hold pending the outcome of this case.

The public equities raised by the defendants simply do not outweigh those offered by the FTC. In addition, given some of the Court's earlier findings, several of the public equities submitted by the defendants are without factual support. For example, the defendants argued that the public equities favor the merger because prices will fall for all products, in all markets, following the merger. Since the Court has already found that the Commission has shown a likelihood of success on the merits with respect to proving that the proposed merger will have anti-competitive effects, the Court cannot give any weight to this particular public equity advanced by the defendants. . . .

Turning finally to the private equities, the defendants have argued that the principal private equity at stake in this case is the loss to Office Depot shareholders who will likely lose a substantial portion of their investments if the merger is enjoined. The Court certainly agrees that Office Depot shareholders may be harmed, at least in the short term, if the Court granted the plaintiff's motion and enjoined the merger. This private equity alone, however, does not suffice to justify denial of a preliminary injunction.

The defendants have also argued that Office Depot itself has suffered a decline since the incipiency of this action. It is clear that Office Depot has lost key personnel, especially in its real estate department. This has hurt this year's projected store openings. The defendants argue, therefore, that Office Depot, as a separate company, will have difficulty competing if the merger is enjoined. While the Court recognizes that Office Depot has indeed been hurt or weakened as an independent stand-alone company, the damage is not irreparable. The evidence shows that Office Depot, which of the three superstores has been the low-priced aggressive maverick of the group, would continue generating sales volume and turning a substantial profit. In reaching this conclusion, the Court credits one of the defendants' own expert witnesses, Steven Mandel, who testified that, in his opinion, Office Depot would be fine even if the merger did not go through. He described Office Depot as a very strong and well-run company, and said that it would certainly have a little bit of a hole to dig out of if the merger were enjoined. However, his ultimate conclusion was that the company would recover. Certainly Office Depot is in a better position to recover and move forward now if the Court grants the plaintiff's motion than it would be if the merger was allowed to go forward and then later the two companies were ordered to separate.

CONCLUSION

Thomas Stemberg pioneered the office supply superstore concept in 1985. He created a deep discount chain selling a broad array of office supplies primarily to small businesses which theretofore were undeniably "paying through the nose" for office supplies. Staples was to be a high volume chain operating at low gross margins, with higher volume leading to still lower costs for consumers. Staples' pricing as well as the pricing of other office supply superstores which soon followed Staples' lead, revolutionized the office products industry, impacting all channels of office products retailing. By selling office products at 30 to 60% off list price, Staples and the other superstores worked as a catalyst that forced everyone else in the industry to focus on cutting their prices. In a relatively short period of time, the office supply superstores caused a general decrease in the price of office products across the board. That decrease continued as the superstores have increased their buying power, forcing manufacturers and suppliers to implement efficiencies in their own businesses in order to compete in the sale of their products.

In light of the undeniable benefits that Staples and Office Depot have brought to consumers, it is with regret that the Court reaches the decision that it must in this case. This decision will most likely kill the merger. The Court feels, to some extent, that the defendants are being punished for their own successes and for the benefits that they have brought to consumers. In effect, they have been hoisted with their own petards. See William Shakespeare, Hamlet, act 3, sc 4. In addition, the Court is concerned with the broader ramifications of this case. The superstore or "category killer" like office supply superstores are a fairly recent phenomenon and certainly not restricted to office supplies. There are a host of superstores or "category killers" in the

Staples ¶527

United States today, covering such areas as pet supplies, home and garden products, bed, bath, and kitchen products, toys, music, books, and electronics. Indeed, such "category killer" stores may be the way of retailing for the future. It remains to be seen if this case is sui generis or is the beginning of a new wave of FTC activism. For these reasons, the Court must emphasize that the ruling in this case is based strictly on the facts of this particular case, and should not be construed as this Court's recognition of general superstore relevant product markets.

Despite the Court's sympathy toward the plight of the defendants in this case, the Court finds that the Commission has shown a "reasonable probability" that the proposed merger between Staples and Office Depot may substantially impair competition and likewise has "raised questions going to the merits so serious, substantial, difficult and doubtful as to make them fair ground for thorough investigation, study, deliberation and determination by the FTC in the first instances and ultimately by the Court of Appeals." Therefore, the Court finds that the Commission has shown a likelihood that it will succeed in proving, after a full administrative trial on the merits, that the effect of the proposed merger between Staples and Office Depot "may be substantially to lessen competition" in violation of Section 7 of the Clayton Act. In addition, the Court has weighed the equities and finds that they tip in favor of granting a preliminary injunction. A preliminary injunction is, therefore, found to be in the public interest. The FTC's motion for a preliminary injunction shall be granted. . . .

Appendix

Antitrust Guidelines for Collaborations Among Competitors

Issued by the
Federal Trade Commission
and the
U.S. Department of Justice

April 2000

ANTITRUST GUIDELINES FOR COLLABORATIONS AMONG COMPETITORS

TABLE OF CONTENTS

PREAMBLE 1

SECTION 1: PURPOSE, DEFINITIONS, AND OVERVIEW 2

1.1 Purpose and Definitions 2

1.2 Overview of Analytical Framework 3

1.3 Competitor Collaborations Distinguished from Mergers 5

SECTION 2: GENERAL PRINCIPLES FOR EVALUATING AGREEMENTS AMONG COMPETITORS 6

2.1 Potential Procompetitive Benefits 6

2.2 Potential Anticompetitive Harms 6

2.3 Analysis of the Overall Collaboration and the Agreements of Which It Consists 7

2.4 Competitive Effects Are Assessed as of the Time of Possible Harm to Competition 7

SECTION 3: ANALYTICAL FRAMEWORK FOR EVALUATING

i

AGREEMENTS AMONG COMPETITORS... 7

3.1 Introduction 7

3.2 Agreements Challenged as Per Se Illegal 8

3.3 Agreements Analyzed under the Rule of Reason 10

    3.31 Nature of the Relevant Agreement: Business Purpose, Operation in the Marketplace and Possible Competitive Concerns 12

        3.31(a) Relevant Agreements that Limit Independent Decision Making or Combine Control or Financial Interests 13

        3.31(b) Relevant Agreements that May Facilitate Collusion 15

    3.32 Relevant Markets Affected by the Collaboration 16

        3.32(a) Goods Markets 16

        3.32(b) Technology Markets 16

        3.32(c) Research and Development: Innovation Markets 17

    3.33 Market Shares and Market Concentration 17

    3.34 Factors Relevant to the Ability and Incentive of the Participants and the Collaboration to Compete 18

        3.34(a) Exclusivity 19

        3.34(b) Control over Assets 19

        3.34(c) Financial Interests in the Collaboration or in Other Participants 20

        3.34(d) Control of the Collaboration's Competitively Significant Decision Making 20

        3.34(e) Likelihood of Anticompetitive Information Sharing 21

		3.34(f) Duration of the Collaboration	21
3.35	Entry		22
3.36	Identifying Procompetitive Benefits of the Collaboration		23
	3.36(a)	Cognizable Efficiencies Must Be Verifiable and Potentially Procompetitive	24
	3.36(b)	Reasonable Necessity and Less Restrictive Alternatives	24
3.37	Overall Competitive Effect		25

SECTION 4: ANTITRUST SAFETY ZONES 25

4.1 Overview 25

4.2 Safety Zone for Competitor Collaborations in General 26

4.3 Safety Zone for Research and Development Competition Analyzed in Terms of Innovation Markets 27

ANTITRUST GUIDELINES FOR COLLABORATIONS AMONG COMPETITORS

PREAMBLE

In order to compete in modern markets, competitors sometimes need to collaborate. Competitive forces are driving firms toward complex collaborations to achieve goals such as expanding into foreign markets, funding expensive innovation efforts, and lowering production and other costs.

Such collaborations often are not only benign but procompetitive. Indeed, in the last two decades, the federal antitrust agencies have brought relatively few civil cases against competitor collaborations. Nevertheless, a perception that antitrust laws are skeptical about agreements among actual or potential competitors may deter the development of procompetitive collaborations.[1]

To provide guidance to business people, the Federal Trade Commission ("FTC") and the U.S. Department of Justice ("DOJ") (collectively, "the Agencies") previously issued guidelines addressing several special circumstances in which antitrust issues related to competitor collaborations may arise.[2] But none of these Guidelines represents a general statement of the Agencies' analytical approach to competitor collaborations. The increasing varieties and use of competitor collaborations have yielded requests for improved clarity regarding their treatment under the antitrust laws.

The new *Antitrust Guidelines for Collaborations among Competitors* ("*Competitor Collaboration Guidelines*") are intended to explain how the Agencies analyze certain antitrust issues raised by collaborations among competitors. Competitor collaborations and the market circumstances in which they operate vary widely. No set of guidelines can provide specific

---

[1] Congress has protected certain collaborations from full antitrust liability by passing the National Cooperative Research Act of 1984 ("NCRA") and the National Cooperative Research and Production Act of 1993 ("NCRPA") (codified together at 15 U.S.C. § § 4301-06).

[2] The *Statements of Antitrust Enforcement Policy in Health Care* ("*Health Care Statements*") outline the Agencies' approach to certain health care collaborations, among other things. The *Antitrust Guidelines for the Licensing of Intellectual Property* ("*Intellectual Property Guidelines*") outline the Agencies' enforcement policy with respect to intellectual property licensing agreements among competitors, among other things. The *1992 DOJ/FTC Horizontal Merger Guidelines*, as amended in 1997 ("*Horizontal Merger Guidelines*"), outline the Agencies' approach to horizontal mergers and acquisitions, and certain competitor collaborations.

answers to every antitrust question that might arise from a competitor collaboration. These Guidelines describe an analytical framework to assist businesses in assessing the likelihood of an antitrust challenge to a collaboration with one or more competitors. They should enable businesses to evaluate proposed transactions with greater understanding of possible antitrust implications, thus encouraging procompetitive collaborations, deterring collaborations likely to harm competition and consumers, and facilitating the Agencies' investigations of collaborations.

SECTION 1: PURPOSE, DEFINITIONS, AND OVERVIEW

1.1 Purpose and Definitions

These Guidelines state the antitrust enforcement policy of the Agencies with respect to competitor collaborations. By stating their general policy, the Agencies hope to assist businesses in assessing whether the Agencies will challenge a competitor collaboration or any of the agreements of which it is comprised.[3] However, these Guidelines cannot remove judgment and discretion in antitrust law enforcement. The Agencies evaluate each case in light of its own facts and apply the analytical framework set forth in these Guidelines reasonably and flexibly.[4]

A "competitor collaboration" comprises a set of one or more agreements, other than merger agreements, between or among competitors to engage in economic activity, and the economic activity resulting therefrom.[5] "Competitors" encompasses both actual and potential competitors.[6] Competitor collaborations involve one or more business activities, such as research and development ("R&D"), production, marketing, distribution, sales or purchasing. Information sharing and various trade association activities also may take place through competitor

---

[3] These Guidelines neither describe how the Agencies litigate cases nor assign burdens of proof or production.

[4] The analytical framework set forth in these Guidelines is consistent with the analytical frameworks in the *Health Care Statements* and the *Intellectual Property Guidelines*, which remain in effect to address issues in their special contexts.

[5] These Guidelines take into account neither the possible effects of competitor collaborations in foreclosing or limiting competition by rivals not participating in a collaboration nor the possible anticompetitive effects of standard setting in the context of competitor collaborations. Nevertheless, these effects may be of concern to the Agencies and may prompt enforcement actions.

[6] Firms also may be in a buyer-seller or other relationship, but that does not eliminate the need to examine the competitor relationship, if present. A firm is treated as a potential competitor if there is evidence that entry by that firm is reasonably probable in the absence of the relevant agreement, or that competitively significant decisions by actual competitors are constrained by concerns that anticompetitive conduct likely would induce the firm to enter.

collaborations.

These Guidelines use the terms "anticompetitive harm," "procompetitive benefit," and "overall competitive effect" in analyzing the competitive effects of agreements among competitors. All of these terms include actual and likely competitive effects. The Guidelines use the term "anticompetitive harm" to refer to an agreement's adverse competitive consequences, without taking account of offsetting procompetitive benefits. Conversely, the term "procompetitive benefit" refers to an agreement's favorable competitive consequences, without taking account of its anticompetitive harm. The terms "overall competitive effect" or "competitive effect" are used in discussing the combination of an agreement's anticompetitive harm and procompetitive benefit.

1.2 Overview of Analytical Framework

Two types of analysis are used by the Supreme Court to determine the lawfulness of an agreement among competitors: per se and rule of reason.[7] Certain types of agreements are so likely to harm competition and to have no significant procompetitive benefit that they do not warrant the time and expense required for particularized inquiry into their effects. Once identified, such agreements are challenged as per se unlawful.[8] All other agreements are evaluated under the rule of reason, which involves a factual inquiry into an agreement's overall competitive effect. As the Supreme Court has explained, rule of reason analysis entails a flexible inquiry and varies in focus and detail depending on the nature of the agreement and market circumstances.[9]

This overview briefly sets forth questions and factors that the Agencies assess in analyzing an agreement among competitors. The rest of the Guidelines should be consulted for the detailed definitions and discussion that underlie this analysis.

Agreements Challenged as Per Se Illegal. Agreements of a type that always or almost always tends to raise price or to reduce output are per se illegal. The Agencies challenge such agreements, once identified, as per se illegal. Types of agreements that have been held per se illegal include agreements among competitors to fix prices or output, rig bids, or share or divide markets by allocating customers, suppliers, territories, or lines of commerce. The courts conclusively presume such agreements, once identified, to be illegal, without inquiring into their claimed business purposes, anticompetitive harms, procompetitive benefits, or overall competitive effects. The Department of Justice prosecutes participants in hard-core cartel agreements criminally.

---

[7] *See* National Soc'y of Prof'l. Eng'rs v. United States, 435 U.S. 679, 692 (1978).

[8] *See* FTC v. Superior Court Trial Lawyers Ass'n, 493 U.S. 411, 432-36 (1990).

[9] *See* California Dental Ass'n v. FTC, 119 S. Ct. 1604, 1617-18 (1999); FTC v. Indiana Fed'n of Dentists, 476 U.S. 447, 459-61 (1986); National Collegiate Athletic Ass'n v. Board of Regents of the Univ. of Okla., 468 U.S. 85, 104-13 (1984).

Agreements Analyzed under the Rule of Reason. Agreements not challenged as per se illegal are analyzed under the rule of reason to determine their overall competitive effect. These include agreements of a type that otherwise might be considered per se illegal, provided they are reasonably related to, and reasonably necessary to achieve procompetitive benefits from, an efficiency-enhancing integration of economic activity.

Rule of reason analysis focuses on the state of competition with, as compared to without, the relevant agreement. The central question is whether the relevant agreement likely harms competition by increasing the ability or incentive profitably to raise price above or reduce output, quality, service, or innovation below what likely would prevail in the absence of the relevant agreement.

Rule of reason analysis entails a flexible inquiry and varies in focus and detail depending on the nature of the agreement and market circumstances. The Agencies focus on only those factors, and undertake only that factual inquiry, necessary to make a sound determination of the overall competitive effect of the relevant agreement. Ordinarily, however, no one factor is dispositive in the analysis.

The Agencies' analysis begins with an examination of the nature of the relevant agreement. As part of this examination, the Agencies ask about the business purpose of the agreement and examine whether the agreement, if already in operation, has caused anticompetitive harm. In some cases, the nature of the agreement and the absence of market power together may demonstrate the absence of anticompetitive harm. In such cases, the Agencies do not challenge the agreement. Alternatively, where the likelihood of anticompetitive harm is evident from the nature of the agreement, or anticompetitive harm has resulted from an agreement already in operation, then, absent overriding benefits that could offset the anticompetitive harm, the Agencies challenge such agreements without a detailed market analysis.

If the initial examination of the nature of the agreement indicates possible competitive concerns, but the agreement is not one that would be challenged without a detailed market analysis, the Agencies analyze the agreement in greater depth. The Agencies typically define relevant markets and calculate market shares and concentration as an initial step in assessing whether the agreement may create or increase market power or facilitate its exercise. The Agencies examine the extent to which the participants and the collaboration have the ability and incentive to compete independently. The Agencies also evaluate other market circumstances, e.g. entry, that may foster or prevent anticompetitive harms.

If the examination of these factors indicates no potential for anticompetitive harm, the Agencies end the investigation without considering procompetitive benefits. If investigation indicates anticompetitive harm, the Agencies examine whether the relevant agreement is reasonably necessary to achieve procompetitive benefits that likely would offset anticompetitive harms.

1.3   Competitor Collaborations Distinguished from Mergers

The competitive effects from competitor collaborations may differ from those of mergers due to a number of factors. Most mergers completely end competition between the merging parties in the relevant market(s). By contrast, most competitor collaborations preserve some form of competition among the participants. This remaining competition may reduce competitive concerns, but also may raise questions about whether participants have agreed to anticompetitive restraints on the remaining competition.

Mergers are designed to be permanent, while competitor collaborations are more typically of limited duration. Thus, participants in a collaboration typically remain potential competitors, even if they are not actual competitors for certain purposes (*e.g.*, R&D) during the collaboration. The potential for future competition between participants in a collaboration requires antitrust scrutiny different from that required for mergers.

Nonetheless, in some cases, competitor collaborations have competitive effects identical to those that would arise if the participants merged in whole or in part. The Agencies treat a competitor collaboration as a horizontal merger in a relevant market and analyze the collaboration pursuant to the *Horizontal Merger Guidelines* if appropriate, which ordinarily is when: (a) the participants are competitors in that relevant market; (b) the formation of the collaboration involves an efficiency-enhancing integration of economic activity in the relevant market; (c) the integration eliminates all competition among the participants in the relevant market; and (d) the collaboration does not terminate within a sufficiently limited period[10] by its own specific and express terms.[11] Effects of the collaboration on competition in other markets are analyzed as appropriate under these Guidelines or other applicable precedent. *See* Example 1.[12]

SECTION 2: GENERAL PRINCIPLES FOR EVALUATING AGREEMENTS AMONG COMPETITORS

2.1 Potential Procompetitive Benefits

---

[10] In general, the Agencies use ten years as a term indicating sufficient permanence to justify treatment of a competitor collaboration as analogous to a merger. The length of this term may vary, however, depending on industry-specific circumstances, such as technology life cycles.

[11] This definition, however, does not determine obligations arising under the Hart-Scott-Rodino Antitrust Improvements Act of 1976, 15 U.S.C. § 18a.

[12] Examples illustrating this and other points set forth in these Guidelines are included in the Appendix.

The Agencies recognize that consumers may benefit from competitor collaborations in a variety of ways. For example, a competitor collaboration may enable participants to offer goods or services that are cheaper, more valuable to consumers, or brought to market faster than would be possible absent the collaboration. A collaboration may allow its participants to better use existing assets, or may provide incentives for them to make output-enhancing investments that would not occur absent the collaboration. The potential efficiencies from competitor collaborations may be achieved through a variety of contractual arrangements including joint ventures, trade or professional associations, licensing arrangements, or strategic alliances.

Efficiency gains from competitor collaborations often stem from combinations of different capabilities or resources. For example, one participant may have special technical expertise that usefully complements another participant's manufacturing process, allowing the latter participant to lower its production cost or improve the quality of its product. In other instances, a collaboration may facilitate the attainment of scale or scope economies beyond the reach of any single participant. For example, two firms may be able to combine their research or marketing activities to lower their cost of bringing their products to market, or reduce the time needed to develop and begin commercial sales of new products. Consumers may benefit from these collaborations as the participants are able to lower prices, improve quality, or bring new products to market faster.

2.2 Potential Anticompetitive Harms

Competitor collaborations may harm competition and consumers by increasing the ability or incentive profitably to raise price above or reduce output, quality, service, or innovation below what likely would prevail in the absence of the relevant agreement. Such effects may arise through a variety of mechanisms. Among other things, agreements may limit independent decision making or combine the control of or financial interests in production, key assets, or decisions regarding price, output, or other competitively sensitive variables, or may otherwise reduce the participants' ability or incentive to compete independently.

Competitor collaborations also may facilitate explicit or tacit collusion through facilitating practices such as the exchange or disclosure of competitively sensitive information or through increased market concentration. Such collusion may involve the relevant market in which the collaboration operates or another market in which the participants in the collaboration are actual or potential competitors.

2.3 Analysis of the Overall Collaboration and the Agreements of Which It Consists

A competitor collaboration comprises a set of one or more agreements, other than merger agreements, between or among competitors to engage in economic activity, and the economic activity resulting therefrom. In general, the Agencies assess the competitive effects of the overall collaboration and any individual agreement or set of agreements within the collaboration that may harm competition. For purposes of these Guidelines, the phrase "relevant agreement" refers to whichever of these three – the overall collaboration, an individual agreement, or a set of agreements – the evaluating Agency is assessing. Two or more agreements are assessed together if their procompetitive benefits or anticompetitive harms are so intertwined that they cannot meaningfully be isolated and attributed to any individual agreement. *See* Example 2.

2.4 Competitive Effects Are Assessed as of the Time of Possible Harm to Competition

The competitive effects of a relevant agreement may change over time, depending on changes in circumstances such as internal reorganization, adoption of new agreements as part of the collaboration, addition or departure of participants, new market conditions, or changes in market share. The Agencies assess the competitive effects of a relevant agreement as of the time of possible harm to competition, whether at formation of the collaboration or at a later time, as appropriate. *See* Example 3. However, an assessment after a collaboration has been formed is sensitive to the reasonable expectations of participants whose significant sunk cost investments in reliance on the relevant agreement were made before it became anticompetitive.

SECTION 3: ANALYTICAL FRAMEWORK FOR EVALUATING AGREEMENTS AMONG COMPETITORS

3.1 Introduction

Section 3 sets forth the analytical framework that the Agencies use to evaluate the competitive effects of a competitor collaboration and the agreements of which it consists. Certain types of agreements are so likely to be harmful to competition and to have no significant benefits that they do not warrant the time and expense required for particularized inquiry into their effects.[13] Once identified, such agreements are challenged as per se illegal.[14]

Agreements not challenged as per se illegal are analyzed under the rule of reason. Rule of reason analysis focuses on the state of competition with, as compared to without, the relevant agreement. Under the rule of reason, the central question is whether the relevant agreement likely harms competition by increasing the ability or incentive profitably to raise price above or reduce output, quality, service, or innovation below what likely would prevail in the absence of the relevant agreement. Given the great variety of competitor collaborations, rule of reason analysis entails a flexible inquiry and varies in focus and detail depending on the nature of the agreement and market circumstances. Rule of reason analysis focuses on only those factors, and undertakes only the degree of factual inquiry, necessary to assess accurately the overall competitive effect of the

---

[13] *See* Continental TV, Inc. v. GTE Sylvania Inc., 433 U.S. 36, 50 n.16 (1977).

[14] *See Superior Court Trial Lawyers Ass'n*, 493 U.S. at 432-36.

relevant agreement.[15]

3.2 Agreements Challenged as Per Se Illegal

Agreements of a type that always or almost always tends to raise price or reduce output are per se illegal.[16] The Agencies challenge such agreements, once identified, as per se illegal. Typically these are agreements not to compete on price or output. Types of agreements that have been held per se illegal include agreements among competitors to fix prices or output, rig bids, or share or divide markets by allocating customers, suppliers, territories or lines of commerce.[17] The courts conclusively presume such agreements, once identified, to be illegal, without inquiring into their claimed business purposes, anticompetitive harms, procompetitive benefits, or overall competitive effects. The Department of Justice prosecutes participants in hard-core cartel agreements criminally.

If, however, participants in an efficiency-enhancing integration of economic activity enter into an agreement that is reasonably related to the integration and reasonably necessary to achieve its procompetitive benefits, the Agencies analyze the agreement under the rule of reason, even if it is of a type that might otherwise be considered per se illegal.[18] See Example 4. In an efficiency-enhancing integration, participants collaborate to perform or cause to be performed (by a joint venture entity created by the collaboration or by one or more participants or by a third party acting on behalf of other participants) one or more business functions, such as production, distribution, marketing, purchasing or R&D, and thereby benefit, or potentially benefit, consumers by expanding output, reducing price, or enhancing quality, service, or innovation. Participants in an efficiency-enhancing integration typically combine, by contract or otherwise, significant capital, technology, or other complementary assets to achieve procompetitive benefits that the participants could not achieve separately. The mere coordination of decisions on price, output, customers, territories, and the like is not integration, and cost savings without integration are not a basis for avoiding per se condemnation. The integration must be of a type that plausibly would generate procompetitive benefits cognizable under the efficiencies analysis set forth in Section 3.36 below. Such procompetitive benefits may enhance the participants' ability or incentives to compete and thus may offset an agreement's anticompetitive tendencies. See Examples 5 through 7.

---

[15] See California Dental Ass'n, 119 S. Ct. at 1617-18; Indiana Fed'n of Dentists, 476 U.S. at 459-61; NCAA, 468 U.S. at 104-13.

[16] See Broadcast Music, Inc. v. Columbia Broadcasting Sys., 441 U.S. 1, 19-20 (1979).

[17] See, e.g., Palmer v. BRG of Georgia, Inc., 498 U.S. 46 (1990) (market allocation); United States v. Trenton Potteries Co., 273 U.S. 392 (1927) (price fixing).

[18] See Arizona v. Maricopa County Medical Soc'y, 457 U.S. 332, 339 n.7, 356-57 (1982) (finding no integration).

An agreement may be "reasonably necessary" without being essential. However, if the participants could achieve an equivalent or comparable efficiency-enhancing integration through practical, significantly less restrictive means, then the Agencies conclude that the agreement is not reasonably necessary.[19] In making this assessment, except in unusual circumstances, the Agencies consider whether practical, significantly less restrictive means were reasonably available when the agreement was entered into, but do not search for a theoretically less restrictive alternative that was not practical given the business realities.

Before accepting a claim that an agreement is reasonably necessary to achieve procompetitive benefits from an integration of economic activity, the Agencies undertake a limited factual inquiry to evaluate the claim.[20] Such an inquiry may reveal that efficiencies from an agreement that are possible in theory are not plausible in the context of the particular collaboration. Some claims – such as those premised on the notion that competition itself is unreasonable – are insufficient as a matter of law,[21] and others may be implausible on their face. In any case, labeling an arrangement a "joint venture" will not protect what is merely a device to raise price or restrict output;[22] the nature of the conduct, not its designation, is determinative.

---

[19] *See id.* at 352-53 (observing that even if a maximum fee schedule for physicians' services were desirable, it was not necessary that the schedule be established by physicians rather than by insurers); *Broadcast Music*, 441 U.S. at 20-21 (setting of price "necessary" for the blanket license).

[20] *See Maricopa*, 457 U.S. at 352-53, 356-57 (scrutinizing the defendant medical foundations for indicia of integration and evaluating the record evidence regarding less restrictive alternatives).

[21] *See Indiana Fed'n of Dentists*, 476 U.S. at 463-64; *NCAA*, 468 U.S. at 116-17; *Prof'l. Eng'rs*, 435 U.S. at 693-96. Other claims, such as an absence of market power, are no defense to per se illegality. *See Superior Court Trial Lawyers Ass'n*, 493 U.S. at 434-36; United States v. Socony-Vacuum Oil Co., 310 U.S. 150, 224-26 & n.59 (1940).

[22] *See* Timken Roller Bearing Co. v. United States, 341 U.S. 593, 598 (1951).

3.3 Agreements Analyzed under the Rule of Reason

Agreements not challenged as per se illegal are analyzed under the rule of reason to determine their overall competitive effect. Rule of reason analysis focuses on the state of competition with, as compared to without, the relevant agreement. The central question is whether the relevant agreement likely harms competition by increasing the ability or incentive profitably to raise price above or reduce output, quality, service, or innovation below what likely would prevail in the absence of the relevant agreement.[23]

Rule of reason analysis entails a flexible inquiry and varies in focus and detail depending on the nature of the agreement and market circumstances.[24] The Agencies focus on only those factors, and undertake only that factual inquiry, necessary to make a sound determination of the overall competitive effect of the relevant agreement. Ordinarily, however, no one factor is dispositive in the analysis.

Under the rule of reason, the Agencies' analysis begins with an examination of the nature of the relevant agreement, since the nature of the agreement determines the types of anticompetitive harms that may be of concern. As part of this examination, the Agencies ask about the business purpose of the agreement and examine whether the agreement, if already in operation, has caused anticompetitive harm.[25] If the nature of the agreement and the absence of market power[26] together demonstrate the absence of anticompetitive harm, the Agencies do not challenge the agreement. *See* Example 8. Alternatively, where the likelihood of anticompetitive harm is evident from the nature of the agreement,[27] or anticompetitive harm has resulted from an agreement

---

[23] In addition, concerns may arise where an agreement increases the ability or incentive of buyers to exercise monopsony power. See *infra* Section 3.31(a).

[24] *See California Dental Ass'n*, 119 S. Ct. at 1612-13, 1617 ("What is required . . . is an enquiry meet for the case, looking to the circumstances, details, and logic of a restraint."); *NCAA*, 468 U.S. 109 n.39 ("the rule of reason can sometimes be applied in the twinkling of an eye") (quoting Phillip E. Areeda, *The "Rule of Reason" in Antitrust Analysis: General Issues* 37-38 (Federal Judicial Center, June 1981)).

[25] *See* Board of Trade of the City of Chicago v. United States, 246 U.S. 231, 238 (1918).

[26] That market power is absent may be determined without defining a relevant market. For example, if no market power is likely under any plausible market definition, it does not matter which one is correct. Alternatively, easy entry may indicate an absence of market power.

[27] *See California Dental Ass'n*, 119 S. Ct. at 1612-13, 1617 (an "obvious anticompetitive effect" would warrant quick condemnation); *Indiana Fed'n of Dentists*, 476 U.S. at 459; *NCAA*, 468 U.S. at 104, 106-10.

already in operation,[28] then, absent overriding benefits that could offset the anticompetitive harm, the Agencies challenge such agreements without a detailed market analysis.[29]

If the initial examination of the nature of the agreement indicates possible competitive concerns, but the agreement is not one that would be challenged without a detailed market analysis, the Agencies analyze the agreement in greater depth. The Agencies typically define relevant markets and calculate market shares and concentration as an initial step in assessing whether the agreement may create or increase market power[30] or facilitate its exercise and thus poses risks to competition.[31] The Agencies examine factors relevant to the extent to which the participants and the collaboration have the ability and incentive to compete independently, such as whether an agreement is exclusive or non-exclusive and its duration.[32] The Agencies also evaluate whether entry would be timely, likely, and sufficient to deter or counteract any anticompetitive harms. In addition, the Agencies assess any other market circumstances that may foster or impede anticompetitive harms.

If the examination of these factors indicates no potential for anticompetitive harm, the Agencies end the investigation without considering procompetitive benefits. If investigation indicates anticompetitive harm, the Agencies examine whether the relevant agreement is reasonably

---

[28] *See Indiana Fed'n of Dentists*, 476 U.S. at 460-61 ("Since the purpose of the inquiries into market definition and market power is to determine whether an arrangement has the potential for genuine adverse effects on competition, 'proof of actual detrimental effects, such as a reduction of output,' can obviate the need for an inquiry into market power, which is but a 'surrogate for detrimental effects.'") (quoting 7 Phillip E. Areeda, *Antitrust Law* ¶ 1511, at 424 (1986)); *NCAA*, 468 U.S. at 104-08, 110 n.42.

[29] *See Indiana Fed'n of Dentists*, 476 U.S. at 459-60 (condemning without "detailed market analysis" an agreement to limit competition by withholding x-rays from patients' insurers after finding no competitive justification).

[30] Market power to a seller is the ability profitably to maintain prices above competitive levels for a significant period of time. Sellers also may exercise market power with respect to significant competitive dimensions other than price, such as quality, service, or innovation. Market power to a buyer is the ability profitably to depress the price paid for a product below the competitive level for a significant period of time and thereby depress output.

[31] *See* Eastman Kodak Co. v. Image Technical Services, Inc., 504 U.S. 451, 464 (1992).

[32] *Compare NCAA*, 468 U.S. at 113-15, 119-20 (noting that colleges were not permitted to televise their own games without restraint), *with Broadcast Music*, 441 U.S. at 23-24 (finding no legal or practical impediment to individual licenses).

necessary to achieve procompetitive benefits that likely would offset anticompetitive harms.[33]

3.31 Nature of the Relevant Agreement: Business Purpose, Operation in the Marketplace and Possible Competitive Concerns

The nature of the agreement is relevant to whether it may cause anticompetitive harm. For example, by limiting independent decision making or combining control over or financial interests in production, key assets, or decisions on price, output, or other competitively sensitive variables, an agreement may create or increase market power or facilitate its exercise by the collaboration, its participants, or both. An agreement to limit independent decision making or to combine control or financial interests may reduce the ability or incentive to compete independently. An agreement also may increase the likelihood of an exercise of market power by facilitating explicit or tacit collusion,[34] either through facilitating practices such as an exchange of competitively sensitive information or through increased market concentration.

In examining the nature of the relevant agreement, the Agencies take into account inferences about business purposes for the agreement that can be drawn from objective facts. The Agencies also consider evidence of the subjective intent of the participants to the extent that it sheds light on competitive effects.[35] The Agencies do not undertake a full analysis of procompetitive benefits pursuant to Section 3.36 below, however, unless an anticompetitive harm appears likely. The Agencies also examine whether an agreement already in operation has caused anticompetitive harm.[36] Anticompetitive harm may be observed, for example, if a competitor collaboration successfully mandates new, anticompetitive conduct or successfully eliminates procompetitive pre-collaboration conduct, such as withholding services that were desired by consumers when offered in a competitive market. If anticompetitive harm is found, examination of market power ordinarily is not required. In some cases, however, a determination of anticompetitive harm may be informed by consideration of market power.

---

[33] See *NCAA*, 468 U.S. at 113-15 (rejecting efficiency claims when production was limited, not enhanced); *Prof'l. Eng'rs*, 435 U.S. at 696 (dictum) (distinguishing restraints that promote competition from those that eliminate competition); *Chicago Bd. of Trade*, 246 U.S. at 238 (same).

[34] As used in these Guidelines, "collusion" is not limited to conduct that involves an agreement under the antitrust laws.

[35] Anticompetitive intent alone does not establish an antitrust violation, and procompetitive intent does not preclude a violation. *See, e.g., Chicago Bd. of Trade*, 246 U.S. at 238. But extrinsic evidence of intent may aid in evaluating market power, the likelihood of anticompetitive harm, and claimed procompetitive justifications where an agreement's effects are otherwise ambiguous.

[36] *See id.*

The following sections illustrate competitive concerns that may arise from the nature of particular types of competitor collaborations. This list is not exhaustive. In addition, where these sections address agreements of a type that otherwise might be considered per se illegal, such as agreements on price, the discussion assumes that the agreements already have been determined to be subject to rule of reason analysis because they are reasonably related to, and reasonably necessary to achieve procompetitive benefits from, an efficiency-enhancing integration of economic activity. *See supra* Section 3.2.

3.31(a) Relevant Agreements that Limit Independent Decision Making or Combine Control or Financial Interests

The following is intended to illustrate but not exhaust the types of agreements that might harm competition by eliminating independent decision making or combining control or financial interests.

Production Collaborations. Competitor collaborations may involve agreements jointly to produce a product sold to others or used by the participants as an input. Such agreements are often procompetitive.[37] Participants may combine complementary technologies, know-how, or other assets to enable the collaboration to produce a good more efficiently or to produce a good that no one participant alone could produce. However, production collaborations may involve agreements on the level of output or the use of key assets, or on the price at which the product will be marketed by the collaboration, or on other competitively significant variables, such as quality, service, or promotional strategies, that can result in anticompetitive harm. Such agreements can create or increase market power or facilitate its exercise by limiting independent decision making or by combining in the collaboration, or in certain participants, the control over some or all production or key assets or decisions about key competitive variables that otherwise would be controlled independently.[38] Such agreements could reduce individual participants' control over assets necessary to compete and thereby reduce their ability to compete independently, combine financial interests in ways that undermine incentives to compete

---

[37] The *NCRPA* accords rule of reason treatment to certain production collaborations. However, the statute permits per se challenges, in appropriate circumstances, to a variety of activities, including agreements to jointly market the goods or services produced or to limit the participants' independent sale of goods or services produced outside the collaboration. *NCRPA*, 15 U.S.C. §§ 4301-02.

[38] For example, where output resulting from a collaboration is transferred to participants for independent marketing, anticompetitive harm could result if that output is restricted or if the transfer takes place at a supracompetitive price. Such conduct could raise participants' marginal costs through inflated per-unit charges on the transfer of the collaboration's output. Anticompetitive harm could occur even if there is vigorous competition among collaboration participants in the output market, since all the participants would have paid the same inflated transfer price.

independently, or both.

Marketing Collaborations. Competitor collaborations may involve agreements jointly to sell, distribute, or promote goods or services that are either jointly or individually produced. Such agreements may be procompetitive, for example, where a combination of complementary assets enables products more quickly and efficiently to reach the marketplace. However, marketing collaborations may involve agreements on price, output, or other competitively significant variables, or on the use of competitively significant assets, such as an extensive distribution network, that can result in anticompetitive harm. Such agreements can create or increase market power or facilitate its exercise by limiting independent decision making; by combining in the collaboration, or in certain participants, control over competitively significant assets or decisions about competitively significant variables that otherwise would be controlled independently; or by combining financial interests in ways that undermine incentives to compete independently. For example, joint promotion might reduce or eliminate comparative advertising, thus harming competition by restricting information to consumers on price and other competitively significant variables.

Buying Collaborations. Competitor collaborations may involve agreements jointly to purchase necessary inputs. Many such agreements do not raise antitrust concerns and indeed may be procompetitive. Purchasing collaborations, for example, may enable participants to centralize ordering, to combine warehousing or distribution functions more efficiently, or to achieve other efficiencies. However, such agreements can create or increase market power (which, in the case of buyers, is called "monopsony power") or facilitate its exercise by increasing the ability or incentive to drive the price of the purchased product, and thereby depress output, below what likely would prevail in the absence of the relevant agreement. Buying collaborations also may facilitate collusion by standardizing participants' costs or by enhancing the ability to project or monitor a participant's output level through knowledge of its input purchases.

Research & Development Collaborations. Competitor collaborations may involve agreements to engage in joint research and development ("R&D"). Most such agreements are procompetitive, and they typically are analyzed under the rule of reason.[39] Through the combination of complementary assets, technology, or know-how, an R&D collaboration may enable participants more quickly or more efficiently to research and develop new or improved goods, services, or production processes. Joint R&D agreements, however, can create or increase market power or facilitate its exercise by limiting independent decision making or by combining in the collaboration, or in certain participants, control over competitively significant assets or all or a portion of participants' individual competitive R&D efforts. Although R&D collaborations also may facilitate tacit collusion on R&D efforts, achieving, monitoring, and punishing departures from collusion is sometimes difficult in the R&D context.

---

[39] Aspects of the antitrust analysis of competitor collaborations involving R&D are governed by provisions of the *NCRPA*, 15 U.S.C. §§ 4301-02.

An exercise of market power may injure consumers by reducing innovation below the level that otherwise would prevail, leading to fewer or no products for consumers to choose from, lower quality products, or products that reach consumers more slowly than they otherwise would. An exercise of market power also may injure consumers by reducing the number of independent competitors in the market for the goods, services, or production processes derived from the R&D collaboration, leading to higher prices or reduced output, quality, or service. A central question is whether the agreement increases the ability or incentive anticompetitively to reduce R&D efforts pursued independently or through the collaboration, for example, by slowing the pace at which R&D efforts are pursued. Other considerations being equal, R&D agreements are more likely to raise competitive concerns when the collaboration or its participants already possess a secure source of market power over an existing product and the new R&D efforts might cannibalize their supracompetitive earnings. In addition, anticompetitive harm generally is more likely when R&D competition is confined to firms with specialized characteristics or assets, such as intellectual property, or when a regulatory approval process limits the ability of late-comers to catch up with competitors already engaged in the R&D.

3.31(b) Relevant Agreements that May Facilitate Collusion

Each of the types of competitor collaborations outlined above can facilitate collusion. Competitor collaborations may provide an opportunity for participants to discuss and agree on anticompetitive terms, or otherwise to collude anticompetitively, as well as a greater ability to detect and punish deviations that would undermine the collusion. Certain marketing, production, and buying collaborations, for example, may provide opportunities for their participants to collude on price, output, customers, territories, or other competitively sensitive variables. R&D collaborations, however, may be less likely to facilitate collusion regarding R&D activities since R&D often is conducted in secret, and it thus may be difficult to monitor an agreement to coordinate R&D. In addition, collaborations can increase concentration in a relevant market and thus increase the likelihood of collusion among all firms, including the collaboration and its participants.

Agreements that facilitate collusion sometimes involve the exchange or disclosure of information. The Agencies recognize that the sharing of information among competitors may be procompetitive and is often reasonably necessary to achieve the procompetitive benefits of certain collaborations; for example, sharing certain technology, know-how, or other intellectual property may be essential to achieve the procompetitive benefits of an R&D collaboration. Nevertheless, in some cases, the sharing of information related to a market in which the collaboration operates or in which the participants are actual or potential competitors may increase the likelihood of collusion on matters such as price, output, or other competitively sensitive variables. The competitive concern depends on the nature of the information shared. Other things being equal, the sharing of information relating to price, output, costs, or strategic planning is more likely to raise competitive concern than the sharing of information relating to less competitively sensitive variables. Similarly, other things being equal, the sharing of information on current operating and future business plans is more likely to raise concerns than the sharing of historical information.

Finally, other things being equal, the sharing of individual company data is more likely to raise concern than the sharing of aggregated data that does not permit recipients to identify individual firm data.

3.32   Relevant Markets Affected by the Collaboration

The Agencies typically identify and assess competitive effects in all of the relevant product and geographic markets in which competition may be affected by a competitor collaboration, although in some cases it may be possible to assess competitive effects directly without defining a particular relevant market(s). Markets affected by a competitor collaboration include all markets in which the economic integration of the participants' operations occurs or in which the collaboration operates or will operate,[40] and may also include additional markets in which any participant is an actual or potential competitor.[41]

3.32(a)   Goods Markets

In general, for goods[42] markets affected by a competitor collaboration, the Agencies approach relevant market definition as described in Section 1 of the *Horizontal Merger Guidelines*. To determine the relevant market, the Agencies generally consider the likely reaction of buyers to a price increase and typically ask, among other things, how buyers would respond to increases over prevailing price levels. However, when circumstances strongly suggest that the prevailing price exceeds what likely would have prevailed absent the relevant agreement, the Agencies use a price more reflective of the price that likely would have prevailed. Once a market has been defined, market shares are assigned both to firms currently in the relevant market and to firms that are able to make "uncommitted" supply responses. *See* Sections 1.31 and 1.32 of the *Horizontal Merger Guidelines*.

3.32(b)   Technology Markets

When rights to intellectual property are marketed separately from the products in which they are used, the Agencies may define technology markets in assessing the competitive effects of a competitor collaboration that includes an agreement to license intellectual property. Technology markets consist of the intellectual property that is licensed and its close substitutes;

---

[40] For example, where a production joint venture buys inputs from an upstream market to incorporate in products to be sold in a downstream market, both upstream and downstream markets may be "markets affected by a competitor collaboration."

[41] Participation in the collaboration may change the participants' behavior in this third category of markets, for example, by altering incentives and available information, or by providing an opportunity to form additional agreements among participants.

[42] The term "goods" also includes services.

that is, the technologies or goods that are close enough substitutes significantly to constrain the exercise of market power with respect to the intellectual property that is licensed. The Agencies approach the definition of a relevant technology market and the measurement of market share as described in Section 3.2.2 of the *Intellectual Property Guidelines*.

3.32(c) Research and Development: Innovation Markets

In many cases, an agreement's competitive effects on innovation are analyzed as a separate competitive effect in a relevant goods market. However, if a competitor collaboration may have competitive effects on innovation that cannot be adequately addressed through the analysis of goods or technology markets, the Agencies may define and analyze an innovation market as described in Section 3.2.3 of the *Intellectual Property Guidelines*. An innovation market consists of the research and development directed to particular new or improved goods or processes and the close substitutes for that research and development. The Agencies define an innovation market only when the capabilities to engage in the relevant research and development can be associated with specialized assets or characteristics of specific firms.

3.33 Market Shares and Market Concentration

Market share and market concentration affect the likelihood that the relevant agreement will create or increase market power or facilitate its exercise. The creation, increase, or facilitation of market power will likely increase the ability and incentive profitably to raise price above or reduce output, quality, service, or innovation below what likely would prevail in the absence of the relevant agreement.

Other things being equal, market share affects the extent to which participants or the collaboration must restrict their own output in order to achieve anticompetitive effects in a relevant market. The smaller the percentage of total supply that a firm controls, the more severely it must restrict its own output in order to produce a given price increase, and the less likely it is that an output restriction will be profitable. In assessing whether an agreement may cause anticompetitive harm, the Agencies typically calculate the market shares of the participants and of the collaboration.[43] The Agencies assign a range of market shares to the collaboration. The high end of that range is the sum of the market shares of the collaboration and its participants. The low end is the share of the collaboration in isolation. In general, the Agencies approach the calculation of market share as set forth in Section 1.4 of the *Horizontal Merger Guidelines*.

Other things being equal, market concentration affects the difficulties and costs of achieving and

---

[43] When the competitive concern is that a limitation on independent decision making or a combination of control or financial interests may yield an anticompetitive reduction of research and development, the Agencies typically frame their inquiries more generally, looking to the strength, scope, and number of competing R&D efforts and their close substitutes. *See supra* Sections 3.31(a) and 3.32(c).

enforcing collusion in a relevant market. Accordingly, in assessing whether an agreement may increase the likelihood of collusion, the Agencies calculate market concentration. In general, the Agencies approach the calculation of market concentration as set forth in Section 1.5 of the *Horizontal Merger Guidelines*, ascribing to the competitor collaboration the same range of market shares described above.

Market share and market concentration provide only a starting point for evaluating the competitive effect of the relevant agreement. The Agencies also examine other factors outlined in the *Horizontal Merger Guidelines* as set forth below:

The Agencies consider whether factors such as those discussed in Section 1.52 of the *Horizontal Merger Guidelines* indicate that market share and concentration data overstate or understate the likely competitive significance of participants and their collaboration.

In assessing whether anticompetitive harm may arise from an agreement that combines control over or financial interests in assets or otherwise limits independent decision making, the Agencies consider whether factors such as those discussed in Section 2.2 of the *Horizontal Merger Guidelines* suggest that anticompetitive harm is more or less likely.

In assessing whether anticompetitive harms may arise from an agreement that may increase the likelihood of collusion, the Agencies consider whether factors such as those discussed in Section 2.1 of the *Horizontal Merger Guidelines* suggest that anticompetitive harm is more or less likely.

In evaluating the significance of market share and market concentration data and interpreting the range of market shares ascribed to the collaboration, the Agencies also examine factors beyond those set forth in the *Horizontal Merger Guidelines*. The following section describes which factors are relevant and the issues that the Agencies examine in evaluating those factors.

3.34 Factors Relevant to the Ability and Incentive of the Participants and the Collaboration to Compete

Competitor collaborations sometimes do not end competition among the participants and the collaboration. Participants may continue to compete against each other and their collaboration, either through separate, independent business operations or through membership in other collaborations. Collaborations may be managed by decision makers independent of the individual participants. Control over key competitive variables may remain outside the collaboration, such as where participants independently market and set prices for the collaboration's output.

Sometimes, however, competition among the participants and the collaboration may be restrained through explicit contractual terms or through financial or other provisions that reduce or eliminate the incentive to compete. The Agencies look to the competitive benefits and harms of the relevant agreement, not merely the formal terms of agreements among the participants.

Where the nature of the agreement and market share and market concentration data reveal a likelihood of anticompetitive harm, the Agencies more closely examine the extent to which the participants and the collaboration have the ability and incentive to compete independent of each other. The Agencies are likely to focus on six factors: (a) the extent to which the relevant agreement is non-exclusive in that participants are likely to continue to compete independently outside the collaboration in the market in which the collaboration operates; (b) the extent to which participants retain independent control of assets necessary to compete; (c) the nature and extent of participants' financial interests in the collaboration or in each other; (d) the control of the collaboration's competitively significant decision making; (e) the likelihood of anticompetitive information sharing; and (f) the duration of the collaboration.

Each of these factors is discussed in further detail below. Consideration of these factors may reduce or increase competitive concern. The analysis necessarily is flexible: the relevance and significance of each factor depends upon the facts and circumstances of each case, and any additional factors pertinent under the circumstances are considered. For example, when an agreement is examined subsequent to formation of the collaboration, the Agencies also examine factual evidence concerning participants' actual conduct.

3.34(a) Exclusivity

The Agencies consider whether, to what extent, and in what manner the relevant agreement permits participants to continue to compete against each other and their collaboration, either through separate, independent business operations or through membership in other collaborations. The Agencies inquire whether a collaboration is non-exclusive in fact as well as in name and consider any costs or other impediments to competing with the collaboration. In assessing exclusivity when an agreement already is in operation, the Agencies examine whether, to what extent, and in what manner participants actually have continued to compete against each other and the collaboration. In general, competitive concern likely is reduced to the extent that participants actually have continued to compete, either through separate, independent business operations or through membership in other collaborations, or are permitted to do so.

3.34(b) Control over Assets

The Agencies ask whether the relevant agreement requires participants to contribute to the collaboration significant assets that previously have enabled or likely would enable participants to be effective independent competitors in markets affected by the collaboration. If such resources must be contributed to the collaboration and are specialized in that they cannot readily be replaced, the participants may have lost all or some of their ability to compete against each other and their collaboration, even if they retain the contractual right to do so.[44] In general, the greater

---

[44] For example, if participants in a production collaboration must contribute most of their productive capacity to the collaboration, the collaboration may impair the ability of its participants to remain effective independent competitors regardless of the terms of the agreement.

the contribution of specialized assets to the collaboration that is required, the less the participants may be relied upon to provide independent competition.

3.34(c) Financial Interests in the Collaboration or in Other Participants

The Agencies assess each participant's financial interest in the collaboration and its potential impact on the participant's incentive to compete independently with the collaboration. The potential impact may vary depending on the size and nature of the financial interest (e.g., whether the financial interest is debt or equity). In general, the greater the financial interest in the collaboration, the less likely is the participant to compete with the collaboration.[45] The Agencies also assess direct equity investments between or among the participants. Such investments may reduce the incentives of the participants to compete with each other. In either case, the analysis is sensitive to the level of financial interest in the collaboration or in another participant relative to the level of the participant's investment in its independent business operations in the markets affected by the collaboration.

3.34(d) Control of the Collaboration's Competitively Significant Decision Making

The Agencies consider the manner in which a collaboration is organized and governed in assessing the extent to which participants and their collaboration have the ability and incentive to compete independently. Thus, the Agencies consider the extent to which the collaboration's governance structure enables the collaboration to act as an independent decision maker. For example, the Agencies ask whether participants are allowed to appoint members of a board of directors for the collaboration, if incorporated, or otherwise to exercise significant control over the operations of the collaboration. In general, the collaboration is less likely to compete independently as participants gain greater control over the collaboration's price, output, and other competitively significant decisions.[46]

To the extent that the collaboration's decision making is subject to the participants' control, the Agencies consider whether that control could be exercised jointly. Joint control over the collaboration's price and output levels could create or increase market power and raise competitive concerns. Depending on the nature of the collaboration, competitive concern also may arise due to joint control over other competitively significant decisions, such as the level and

---

[45] Similarly, a collaboration's financial interest in a participant may diminish the collaboration's incentive to compete with that participant.

[46] Control may diverge from financial interests. For example, a small equity investment may be coupled with a right to veto large capital expenditures and, thereby, to effectively limit output. The Agencies examine a collaboration's actual governance structure in assessing issues of control.

scope of R&D efforts and investment. In contrast, to the extent that participants independently set the price and quantity [47] of their share of a collaboration's output and independently control other competitively significant decisions, an agreement's likely anticompetitive harm is reduced.[48]

3.34(e) Likelihood of Anticompetitive Information Sharing

The Agencies evaluate the extent to which competitively sensitive information concerning markets affected by the collaboration likely would be disclosed. This likelihood depends on, among other things, the nature of the collaboration, its organization and governance, and safeguards implemented to prevent or minimize such disclosure. For example, participants might refrain from assigning marketing personnel to an R&D collaboration, or, in a marketing collaboration, participants might limit access to competitively sensitive information regarding their respective operations to only certain individuals or to an independent third party. Similarly, a buying collaboration might use an independent third party to handle negotiations in which its participants' input requirements or other competitively sensitive information could be revealed. In general, it is less likely that the collaboration will facilitate collusion on competitively sensitive variables if appropriate safeguards governing information sharing are in place.

3.34(f) Duration of the Collaboration

The Agencies consider the duration of the collaboration in assessing whether participants retain the ability and incentive to compete against each other and their collaboration. In general, the shorter the duration, the more likely participants are to compete against each other and their collaboration.

3.35 Entry

Easy entry may deter or prevent profitably maintaining price above, or output, quality, service or innovation below, what likely would prevail in the absence of the relevant agreement. Where the nature of the agreement and market share and concentration data suggest a likelihood of anticompetitive harm that is not sufficiently mitigated by any continuing competition identified

---

[47] Even if prices to consumers are set independently, anticompetitive harms may still occur if participants jointly set the collaboration's level of output. For example, participants may effectively coordinate price increases by reducing the collaboration's level of output and collecting their profits through high transfer prices, *i.e.*, through the amounts that participants contribute to the collaboration in exchange for each unit of the collaboration's output. Where a transfer price is determined by reference to an objective measure not under the control of the participants, (*e.g.*, average price in a different unconcentrated geographic market), competitive concern may be less likely.

[48] Anticompetitive harm also is less likely if individual participants may independently increase the overall output of the collaboration.

through the analysis in Section 3.34, the Agencies inquire whether entry would be timely, likely, and sufficient in its magnitude, character and scope to deter or counteract the anticompetitive harm of concern. If so, the relevant agreement ordinarily requires no further analysis.

As a general matter, the Agencies assess timeliness, likelihood, and sufficiency of committed entry under principles set forth in Section 3 of the *Horizontal Merger Guidelines*.[49] However, unlike mergers, competitor collaborations often restrict only certain business activities, while preserving competition among participants in other respects, and they may be designed to terminate after a limited duration. Consequently, the extent to which an agreement creates and enables identification of opportunities that would induce entry and the conditions under which ease of entry may deter or counteract anticompetitive harms may be more complex and less direct than for mergers and will vary somewhat according to the nature of the relevant agreement. For example, the likelihood of entry may be affected by what potential entrants believe about the probable duration of an anticompetitive agreement. Other things being equal, the shorter the anticipated duration of an anticompetitive agreement, the smaller the profit opportunities for potential entrants, and the lower the likelihood that it will induce committed entry. Examples of other differences are set forth below.

For certain collaborations, sufficiency of entry may be affected by the possibility that entrants will participate in the anticompetitive agreement. To the extent that such participation raises the amount of entry needed to deter or counteract anticompetitive harms, and assets required for entry are not adequately available for entrants to respond fully to their sales opportunities, or otherwise renders entry inadequate in magnitude, character or scope, sufficient entry may be more difficult to achieve.[50]

---

[49] Committed entry is defined as new competition that requires expenditure of significant sunk costs of entry and exit. *See* Section 3.0 of the *Horizontal Merger Guidelines*.

[50] Under the same principles applied to production and marketing collaborations, the exercise of monopsony power by a buying collaboration may be deterred or counteracted by the entry of new purchasers. To the extent that collaborators reduce their purchases, they may create an opportunity for new buyers to make purchases without forcing the price of the input above pre-relevant agreement levels. Committed purchasing entry, defined as new purchasing competition that requires expenditure of significant sunk costs of entry and exit — such as a new steel factory built in response to a reduction in the price of iron ore — is analyzed under principles analogous to those articulated in Section 3 of the *Horizontal Merger Guidelines*. Under that analysis, the Agencies assess whether a monopsonistic price reduction is likely to attract committed purchasing entry, profitable at pre-relevant agreement prices, that would not have occurred before the relevant agreement at those same prices. (Uncommitted new buyers are identified as participants in the relevant market if their demand responses to a price decrease are likely to occur within one year and without the expenditure of significant sunk costs of entry and exit. *See id.* at Sections 1.32 and 1.41.)

In the context of research and development collaborations, widespread availability of R&D capabilities and the large gains that may accrue to successful innovators often suggest a high likelihood that entry will deter or counteract anticompetitive reductions of R&D efforts. Nonetheless, such conditions do not always pertain, and the Agencies ask whether entry may deter or counteract anticompetitive R&D reductions, taking into account the likelihood, timeliness, and sufficiency of entry.

To be timely, entry must be sufficiently prompt to deter or counteract such harms. The Agencies evaluate the likelihood of entry based on the extent to which potential entrants have (1) core competencies (and the ability to acquire any necessary specialized assets) that give them the ability to enter into competing R&D and (2) incentives to enter into competing R&D. The sufficiency of entry depends on whether the character and scope of the entrants' R&D efforts are close enough to the reduced R&D efforts to be likely to achieve similar innovations in the same time frame or otherwise to render a collaborative reduction of R&D unprofitable.

3.36 Identifying Procompetitive Benefits of the Collaboration

Competition usually spurs firms to achieve efficiencies internally. Nevertheless, as explained above, competitor collaborations have the potential to generate significant efficiencies that benefit consumers in a variety of ways. For example, a competitor collaboration may enable firms to offer goods or services that are cheaper, more valuable to consumers, or brought to market faster than would otherwise be possible. Efficiency gains from competitor collaborations often stem from combinations of different capabilities or resources. *See supra* Section 2.1. Indeed, the primary benefit of competitor collaborations to the economy is their potential to generate such efficiencies.

Efficiencies generated through a competitor collaboration can enhance the ability and incentive of the collaboration and its participants to compete, which may result in lower prices, improved quality, enhanced service, or new products. For example, through collaboration, competitors may be able to produce an input more efficiently than any one participant could individually; such collaboration-generated efficiencies may enhance competition by permitting two or more ineffective (*e.g.*, high cost) participants to become more effective, lower cost competitors. Even when efficiencies generated through a competitor collaboration enhance the collaboration's or the participants' ability to compete, however, a competitor collaboration may have other effects that may lessen competition and ultimately may make the relevant agreement anticompetitive.

If the Agencies conclude that the relevant agreement has caused, or is likely to cause, anticompetitive harm, they consider whether the agreement is reasonably necessary to achieve "cognizable efficiencies." "Cognizable efficiencies" are efficiencies that have been verified by the Agencies, that do not arise from anticompetitive reductions in output or service, and that cannot be achieved through practical, significantly less restrictive means. *See infra* Sections 3.36(a) and 3.36(b). Cognizable efficiencies are assessed net of costs produced by the competitor collaboration or incurred in achieving those efficiencies.

3.36(a) Cognizable Efficiencies Must Be Verifiable and Potentially Procompetitive

Efficiencies are difficult to verify and quantify, in part because much of the information relating to efficiencies is uniquely in the possession of the collaboration's participants. The participants must substantiate efficiency claims so that the Agencies can verify by reasonable means the likelihood and magnitude of each asserted efficiency; how and when each would be achieved; any costs of doing so; how each would enhance the collaboration's or its participants' ability and incentive to compete; and why the relevant agreement is reasonably necessary to achieve the claimed efficiencies (*see* Section 3.36 (b)). Efficiency claims are not considered if they are vague or speculative or otherwise cannot be verified by reasonable means.

Moreover, cognizable efficiencies must be potentially procompetitive. Some asserted efficiencies, such as those premised on the notion that competition itself is unreasonable, are insufficient as a matter of law. Similarly, cost savings that arise from anticompetitive output or service reductions are not treated as cognizable efficiencies. *See* Example 9.

3.36(b) Reasonable Necessity and Less Restrictive Alternatives

The Agencies consider only those efficiencies for which the relevant agreement is reasonably necessary. An agreement may be "reasonably necessary" without being essential. However, if the participants could have achieved or could achieve similar efficiencies by practical, significantly less restrictive means, then the Agencies conclude that the relevant agreement is not reasonably necessary to their achievement. In making this assessment, the Agencies consider only alternatives that are practical in the business situation faced by the participants; the Agencies do not search for a theoretically less restrictive alternative that is not realistic given business realities.

The reasonable necessity of an agreement may depend upon the market context and upon the duration of the agreement. An agreement that may be justified by the needs of a new entrant, for example, may not be reasonably necessary to achieve cognizable efficiencies in different market circumstances. The reasonable necessity of an agreement also may depend on whether it deters individual participants from undertaking free riding or other opportunistic conduct that could reduce significantly the ability of the collaboration to achieve cognizable efficiencies. Collaborations sometimes include agreements to discourage any one participant from appropriating an undue share of the fruits of the collaboration or to align participants' incentives to encourage cooperation in achieving the efficiency goals of the collaboration. The Agencies assess whether such agreements are reasonably necessary to deter opportunistic conduct that otherwise would likely prevent the achievement of cognizable efficiencies. *See* Example 10.

3.37 Overall Competitive Effect

If the relevant agreement is reasonably necessary to achieve cognizable efficiencies, the Agencies assess the likelihood and magnitude of cognizable efficiencies and anticompetitive harms to determine the agreement's overall actual or likely effect on competition in the relevant market. To make the requisite determination, the Agencies consider whether cognizable efficiencies likely would be sufficient to offset the potential of the agreement to harm consumers in the relevant market, for example, by preventing price increases.[51]

The Agencies' comparison of cognizable efficiencies and anticompetitive harms is necessarily an approximate judgment. In assessing the overall competitive effect of an agreement, the Agencies consider the magnitude and likelihood of both the anticompetitive harms and cognizable efficiencies from the relevant agreement. The likelihood and magnitude of anticompetitive harms in a particular case may be insignificant compared to the expected cognizable efficiencies, or vice versa. As the expected anticompetitive harm of the agreement increases, the Agencies require evidence establishing a greater level of expected cognizable efficiencies in order to avoid the conclusion that the agreement will have an anticompetitive effect overall. When the anticompetitive harm of the agreement is likely to be particularly large, extraordinarily great cognizable efficiencies would be necessary to prevent the agreement from having an anticompetitive effect overall.

SECTION 4: ANTITRUST SAFETY ZONES

4.1 Overview

Because competitor collaborations are often procompetitive, the Agencies believe that "safety zones" are useful in order to encourage such activity. The safety zones set out below are designed to provide participants in a competitor collaboration with a degree of certainty in those situations in which anticompetitive effects are so unlikely that the Agencies presume the arrangements to be lawful without inquiring into particular circumstances. They are not intended to discourage competitor collaborations that fall outside the safety zones.

The Agencies emphasize that competitor collaborations are not anticompetitive merely because they fall outside the safety zones. Indeed, many competitor collaborations falling outside the safety zones are procompetitive or competitively neutral. The Agencies analyze arrangements outside the safety zones based on the principles outlined in Section 3 above.

The following sections articulate two safety zones. Section 4.2 sets out a general safety zone

---

[51] In most cases, the Agencies' enforcement decisions depend on their analysis of the overall effect of the relevant agreement over the short term. The Agencies also will consider the effects of cognizable efficiencies with no short-term, direct effect on prices in the relevant market. Delayed benefits from the efficiencies (due to delay in the achievement of, or the realization of consumer benefits from, the efficiencies) will be given less weight because they are less proximate and more difficult to predict.

applicable to any competitor collaboration.[52] Section 4.3 establishes a safety zone applicable to research and development collaborations whose competitive effects are analyzed within an innovation market. These safety zones are intended to supplement safety zone provisions in the Agencies' other guidelines and statements of enforcement policy.[53]

4.2 Safety Zone for Competitor Collaborations in General

Absent extraordinary circumstances, the Agencies do not challenge a competitor collaboration when the market shares of the collaboration and its participants collectively account for no more than twenty percent of each relevant market in which competition may be affected.[54] The safety zone, however, does not apply to agreements that are per se illegal, or that would be challenged without a detailed market analysis,[55] or to competitor collaborations to which a merger analysis is applied.[56]

4.3 Safety Zone for Research and Development Competition Analyzed in Terms of Innovation Markets

Absent extraordinary circumstances, the Agencies do not challenge a competitor collaboration on the basis of effects on competition in an innovation market where three or more independently controlled research efforts in addition to those of the collaboration possess the required

---

[52] *See* Sections 1.1 and 1.3 above.

[53] The Agencies have articulated antitrust safety zones in *Health Care Statements* 7 & 8 and the *Intellectual Property Guidelines*, as well as in the *Horizontal Merger Guidelines*. The antitrust safety zones in these other guidelines relate to particular facts in a specific industry or to particular types of transactions.

[54] For purposes of the safety zone, the Agencies consider the combined market shares of the participants and the collaboration. For example, with a collaboration among two competitors where each participant individually holds a 6 percent market share in the relevant market and the collaboration separately holds a 3 percent market share in the relevant market, the combined market share in the relevant market for purposes of the safety zone would be 15 percent. This collaboration, therefore, would fall within the safety zone. However, if the collaboration involved three competitors, each with a 6 percent market share in the relevant market, the combined market share in the relevant market for purposes of the safety zone would be 21 percent, and the collaboration would fall outside the safety zone. Including market shares of the participants takes into account possible spillover effects on competition within the relevant market among the participants and their collaboration.

[55] *See supra* notes 27-29 and accompanying text in Section 3.3.

[56] *See* Section 1.3 above.

specialized assets or characteristics and the incentive to engage in R&D that is a close substitute for the R&D activity of the collaboration. In determining whether independently controlled R&D efforts are close substitutes, the Agencies consider, among other things, the nature, scope, and magnitude of the R&D efforts; their access to financial support; their access to intellectual property, skilled personnel, or other specialized assets; their timing; and their ability, either acting alone or through others, to successfully commercialize innovations. The antitrust safety zone does not apply to agreements that are per se illegal, or that would be challenged without a detailed market analysis,[57] or to competitor collaborations to which a merger analysis is applied.[58]

---

[57] *See supra* notes 27-29 and accompanying text in Section 3.3.

[58] *See* Section 1.3 above.

Appendix

Section 1.3

Example 1 (Competitor Collaboration/Merger)

Facts

Two oil companies agree to integrate all of their refining and refined product marketing operations. Under terms of the agreement, the collaboration will expire after twelve years; prior to that expiration date, it may be terminated by either participant on six months' prior notice. The two oil companies maintain separate crude oil production operations.

Analysis

The formation of the collaboration involves an efficiency-enhancing integration of operations in the refining and refined product markets, and the integration eliminates all competition between the participants in those markets. The evaluating Agency likely would conclude that expiration after twelve years does not constitute termination "within a sufficiently limited period." The participants' entitlement to terminate the collaboration at any time after giving prior notice is not termination by the collaboration's "own specific and express terms." Based on the facts presented, the evaluating Agency likely would analyze the collaboration under the *Horizontal Merger Guidelines*, rather than as a competitor collaboration under these Guidelines. Any agreements restricting competition on crude oil production would be analyzed under these Guidelines.

Section 2.3

Example 2 (Analysis of Individual Agreements/Set of Agreements)

Facts

Two firms enter a joint venture to develop and produce a new software product to be sold independently by the participants. The product will be useful in two areas, biotechnology research and pharmaceuticals research, but doing business with each of the two classes of purchasers would require a different distribution network and a separate marketing campaign. Successful penetration of one market is likely to stimulate sales in the other by enhancing the reputation of the software and by facilitating the ability of biotechnology and pharmaceutical researchers to use the fruits of each other's efforts. Although the software is to be marketed independently by the participants rather than by the joint venture, the participants agree that one will sell only to biotechnology researchers and the other will sell only to pharmaceutical researchers. The participants also agree to fix the maximum price that either firm may charge. The parties assert that the combination of these two requirements is necessary for the successful marketing of the new product. They argue that the market allocation provides each participant with adequate incentives to commercialize the product in its sector without fear that the other participant will free-ride on its efforts and that the maximum price prevents either participant from unduly exploiting its sector of the market to the detriment of sales efforts in the other sector.

Analysis

The evaluating Agency would assess overall competitive effects associated with the collaboration in its entirety and with individual agreements, such as the agreement to allocate markets, the agreement to fix maximum prices, and any of the sundry other agreements associated with joint development and production and independent marketing of the software. From the facts presented, it appears that the agreements to allocate markets and to fix maximum prices may be so intertwined that their benefits and harms "cannot meaningfully be isolated." The two agreements arguably operate together to ensure a particular blend of incentives to achieve the potential procompetitive benefits of successful commercialization of the new product. Moreover, the effects of the agreement to fix maximum prices may mitigate the price effects of the agreement to allocate markets. Based on the facts presented, the evaluating Agency likely would conclude that the agreements to allocate markets and to fix maximum prices should be analyzed as a whole.

Section 2.4

Example 3 (Time of Possible Harm to Competition)

Facts

A group of 25 small-to-mid-size banks formed a joint venture to establish an automatic teller machine network. To ensure sufficient business to justify launching the venture, the joint venture agreement specified that participants would not participate in any other ATM networks. Numerous other ATM networks were forming in roughly the same time period.

Over time, the joint venture expanded by adding more and more banks, and the number of its competitors fell. Now, ten years after formation, the joint venture has 900 member banks and controls 60% of the ATM outlets in a relevant geographic market. Following complaints from consumers that ATM fees have rapidly escalated, the evaluating Agency assesses the rule barring participation in other ATM networks, which now binds 900 banks.

Analysis

The circumstances in which the venture operates have changed over time, and the evaluating Agency would determine whether the exclusivity rule now harms competition. In assessing the exclusivity rule's competitive effect, the evaluating Agency would take account of the collaboration's substantial current market share and any procompetitive benefits of exclusivity under present circumstances, along with other factors discussed in Section 3. The Agencies would consider whether significant sunk investments were made in reliance on the exclusivity rule.

Section 3.2

Example 4 (Agreement Not to Compete on Price)

Facts

Net-Business and Net-Company are two start-up companies. They independently developed, and have begun selling in competition with one another, software for the networks that link users within a particular business to each other and, in some cases, to entities outside the business. Both Net-Business and Net-Company were formed by computer specialists with no prior business expertise, and they are having trouble implementing marketing strategies, distributing their inventory, and managing their sales forces. The two companies decide to form a partnership joint venture, NET-FIRM, whose sole function will be to market and distribute the network software products of Net-Business and Net-Company. NET-FIRM will be the exclusive marketer of network software produced by Net-Business and Net-Company. Net-Business and Net-Company will each have 50% control of NET-FIRM, but each will derive profits from NET-FIRM in proportion to the revenues from sales of that partner's products. The documents setting up NET-FIRM specify that Net-Business and Net-Company will agree on the prices for the products that NET-FIRM will sell.

Analysis

Net-Business and Net-Company will agree on the prices at which NET-FIRM will sell their individually-produced software. The agreement is one "not to compete on price," and it is of a type that always or almost always tends to raise price or reduce output. The agreement to jointly set price may be challenged as per se illegal, unless it is reasonably related to, and reasonably necessary to achieve procompetitive benefits from, an efficiency-enhancing integration of economic activity.

Example 5 (Specialization without Integration)

Facts

Firm A and Firm B are two of only three producers of automobile carburetors. Minor engine variations from year to year, even within given models of a particular automobile manufacturer, require re-design of each year's carburetor and re-tooling for carburetor production. Firms A and B meet and agree that henceforth Firm A will design and produce carburetors only for automobile models of even-numbered years and Firm B will design and produce carburetors only for automobile models of odd-numbered years. Some design and re-tooling costs would be saved, but automobile manufacturers would face only two suppliers each year, rather than three.

Analysis

The agreement allocates sales by automobile model year and constitutes an agreement "not to compete on . . . output." The participants do not combine production; rather, the collaboration consists solely of an agreement *not* to produce certain carburetors. The mere coordination of decisions on output is not integration, and cost-savings without integration, such as the costs saved by refraining from design and production for any given model year, are not a basis for avoiding per se condemnation. The agreement is of a type so likely to harm competition and to have no significant benefits that particularized inquiry into its competitive effect is deemed by the antitrust laws not to be worth the time and expense that would be required. Consequently, the evaluating Agency likely would conclude that the agreement is per se illegal.

Example 6 (Efficiency-Enhancing Integration Present)

Facts

Compu-Max and Compu-Pro are two major producers of a variety of computer software. Each has a large, world-wide sales department. Each firm has developed and sold its own word-processing software. However, despite all efforts to develop a strong market presence in word processing, each firm has achieved only slightly more than a 10% market share, and neither is a major competitor to the two firms that dominate the word-processing software market.

Compu-Max and Compu-Pro determine that in light of their complementary areas of design expertise they could develop a markedly better word-processing program together than either can produce on its own. Compu-Max and Compu-Pro form a joint venture, WORD-FIRM, to jointly develop and market a new word-processing program, with expenses and profits to be split equally. Compu-Max and Compu-Pro both contribute to WORD-FIRM software developers experienced with word processing.

Analysis

Compu-Max and Compu-Pro have combined their word-processing design efforts, reflecting complementary areas of design expertise, in a common endeavor to develop new word-processing software that they could not have developed separately. Each participant has contributed significant assets – the time and know-how of its word-processing software developers – to the joint effort. Consequently, the evaluating Agency likely would conclude that the joint word-processing software development project is an efficiency-enhancing integration of economic activity that promotes procompetitive benefits.

Example 7 (Efficiency-Enhancing Integration Absent)

Facts

Each of the three major producers of flashlight batteries has a patent on a process for manufacturing a revolutionary new flashlight battery -- the Century Battery -- that would last 100 years without requiring recharging or replacement. There is little chance that another firm could produce such a battery without infringing one of the patents. Based on consumer surveys, each firm believes that aggregate profits will be less if all three sold the Century Battery than if all three sold only conventional batteries, but that any one firm could maximize profits by being the first to introduce a Century Battery. All three are capable of introducing the Century Battery within two years, although it is uncertain who would be first to market.

One component in all conventional batteries is a copper widget. An essential element in each producers' Century Battery would be a zinc, rather than a copper widget. Instead of introducing the Century Battery, the three producers agree that their batteries will use only copper widgets. Adherence to the agreement precludes any of the producers from introducing a Century Battery.

Analysis

The agreement to use only copper widgets is merely an agreement not to produce any zinc-based batteries, in particular, the Century Battery. It is "an agreement not to compete on . . . output" and is "of a type that always or almost always tends to raise price or reduce output." The participants do not collaborate to perform any business functions, and there are no procompetitive benefits from an efficiency-enhancing integration of economic activity. The evaluating Agency likely would challenge the agreement to use only copper widgets as per se illegal.

Section 3.3

Example 8 (Rule-of-Reason: Agreement Quickly Exculpated)

Facts

Under the facts of Example 4, Net-Business and Net-Company jointly market their independently-produced network software products through NET-FIRM. Those facts are changed in one respect: rather than jointly setting the prices of their products, Net-Business and Net-Company will each independently specify the prices at which its products are to be sold by NET-FIRM. The participants explicitly agree that each company will decide on the prices for its own software independently of the other company. The collaboration also includes a requirement that NET-FIRM compile and transmit to each participant quarterly reports summarizing any comments received from customers in the course of NET-FIRM's marketing efforts regarding the desirable/undesirable features of and desirable improvements to (1) that participant's product and (2) network software in general. Sufficient provisions are included to prevent the company-specific information reported to one participant from being disclosed to the other, and those provisions are followed. The information pertaining to network software in general is to be reported simultaneously to both participants.

Analysis

Under these revised facts, there is no agreement "not to compete on price or output." Absent any agreement of a type that always or almost always tends to raise price or reduce output, and absent any subsequent conduct suggesting that the firms did not follow their explicit agreement to set prices independently, no aspect of the partnership arrangement might be subjected to per se analysis. Analysis would continue under the rule of reason.

The information disclosure arrangements provide for the sharing of a very limited category of information: customer-response data pertaining to network software in general. Collection and sharing of information of this nature is unlikely to increase the ability or incentive of Net-Business or Net-Company to raise price or reduce output, quality, service, or innovation. There is no evidence that the disclosure arrangements have caused anticompetitive harm and no evidence that the prohibitions against disclosure of firm-specific information have been violated. Under any plausible relevant market definition, Net-Business and Net-Company have small market shares, and there is no other evidence to suggest that they have market power. In light of these facts, the evaluating Agency would refrain from further investigation.

Section 3.36(a)

Example 9 (Cost Savings from Anticompetitive Output or Service Reductions)

Facts

Two widget manufacturers enter a marketing collaboration. Each will continue to manufacture and set the price for its own widget, but the widgets will be promoted by a joint sales force. The two manufacturers conclude that through this collaboration they can increase their profits using only half of their aggregate pre-collaboration sales forces by (1) taking advantage of economies of scale -- presenting both widgets during the same customer call -- and (2) refraining from time-consuming demonstrations highlighting the relative advantages of one manufacturer's widgets over the other manufacturer's widgets. Prior to their collaboration, both manufacturers had engaged in the demonstrations.

Analysis

The savings attributable to economies of scale would be cognizable efficiencies. In contrast, eliminating demonstrations that highlight the relative advantages of one manufacturer's widgets over the other manufacturer's widgets deprives customers of information useful to their decision making. Cost savings from this source arise from an anticompetitive output or service reduction and would not be cognizable efficiencies.

Section 3.36(b)

Example 10 (Efficiencies from Restrictions on Competitive Independence)

Facts

Under the facts of Example 6, Compu-Max and Compu-Pro decide to collaborate on developing and marketing word-processing software. The firms agree that neither one will engage in R&D for designing word-processing software outside of their WORD-FIRM joint venture. Compu-Max papers drafted during the negotiations cite the concern that absent a restriction on outside word-processing R&D, Compu-Pro might withhold its best ideas, use the joint venture to learn Compu-Max's approaches to design problems, and then use that information to design an improved word-processing software product on its own. Compu-Pro's files contain similar documents regarding Compu-Max.

Compu-Max and Compu-Pro further agree that neither will sell its previously designed word-processing program once their jointly developed product is ready to be introduced. Papers in both firms' files, dating from the time of the negotiations, state that this latter restraint was designed to foster greater trust between the participants and thereby enable the collaboration to function more smoothly. As further support, the parties point to a recent failed collaboration involving other firms who sought to collaborate on developing and selling a new spread-sheet program while independently marketing their older spread-sheet software.

Analysis

The restraints on outside R&D efforts and on outside sales both restrict the competitive independence of the participants and could cause competitive harm. The evaluating Agency would inquire whether each restraint is reasonably necessary to achieve cognizable efficiencies. In the given context, that inquiry would entail an assessment of whether, by aligning the participants' incentives, the restraints in fact are reasonably necessary to deter opportunistic conduct that otherwise would likely prevent achieving cognizable efficiency goals of the collaboration.

With respect to the limitation on independent R&D efforts, possible alternatives might include agreements specifying the level and quality of each participant's R&D contributions to WORD-FIRM or requiring the sharing of all relevant R&D. The evaluating Agency would assess whether any alternatives would permit each participant to adequately monitor the scope and quality of the other's R&D contributions and whether they would effectively prevent the misappropriation of the other participant's know-how. In some circumstances, there may be no "practical, significantly less restrictive" alternative.

Although the agreement prohibiting outside sales might be challenged as per se illegal if not reasonably necessary for achieving the procompetitive benefits of the integration discussed in Example 6, the evaluating Agency likely would analyze the agreement under the rule of reason if it could not adequately assess the claim of reasonable necessity through limited factual inquiry. As a general matter, participants' contributions of marketing assets to the collaboration could more readily be monitored than their contributions of know-how, and neither participant may be capable of misappropriating the other's marketing contributions as readily as it could misappropriate know-how. Consequently, the specification and monitoring of each participant's marketing contributions could be a "practical, significantly less restrictive" alternative to prohibiting outside sales of pre-existing products. The evaluating Agency, however, would examine the experiences of the failed spread-sheet collaboration and any other facts presented by the parties to better assess whether such specification and monitoring would likely enable the achievement of cognizable efficiencies.